SPECIAL UNITS
ASSAULT POLICE

Illustrations: Octavio Díez Cámara, Grupo Especial de Operaciones,
Nucleo Operativo Centrale di Sicurezza, Sección Fuerzas Especiales and
Utvar Rychleho Nasazeni.

Production: Lema Publications, S.L.
Director: Josep M. Parramón Homs
Text: Octavio Díez Cámara
Editor: Eva Mª Durán
Cordinator: Eduardo Hernández
Layout: Rakel Medina

© Lema Publications, S.L. 2000

ISBN 84-95323-41-9

Photocromes and phototypesetting: Novasis, S.A.
Barcelona (Spain)
Printed in Spain

SPECIAL UNITS
ASSAULT POLICE

GEO: SPANISH POLICE CORPS ASSAULT GROUP

Terrorist groups, drug trafficking networks, organized crime groups or kidnappers are the principle targets of action taken by the Special Operations Group (Grupo Especial de Operaciones, or GEO) of the Spanish National Police Corps. This group is specially prepared for assault and detentions requiring highly trained personnel and the use of special techniques.

The personnel's training, capacity for action and potential for use have been demonstrated in numerous highly effective operations conducted since the group was created more than two decades ago.

Need for antiterrorist action

The lack of a police-type, special operations group in Spain that could deal with terrorist attacks led Captain Ernesto García-Quijada Romero to draw up a report on Spain's specific needs and possible solutions. In November of 1977, as a consequence of the information contained therein, the first positions were offered to constitute the GEO, with the principle mission of combating active terrorist groups.

Protective gear
When GEO officers carry out the missions they are entrusted, they normally wear thick, bullet-proof vests protecting their torsos, a strong helmet designed to withstand diverse types of bullets, and a gas mask with a cartridge to filter exhaled air.

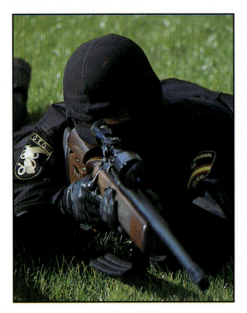

Approximately 400 police officers applied for the position. They were subject to medical, physical, intelligence and psychological tests directed by Captains Ernesto García-Quijada and Juan Senso Galán. A total of 70 police officers were selected as candidates to cover the 50 positions available.

Activation and background

The candidates and teaching staff met at a barracks belonging to the Armed Police Force of Guadalajara, where training began in such areas as shooting, physical training, personal defense, swimming, explosives, parachuting with automatic

Snipers
Snipers such as this officer, holding a Sig SSG-2000 .308 Winchester lock rifle, are prepared to neutralize any target within the range of this weapon, which is approximately 600 m, with a single shot.

GEO: SPANISH POLICE CORPS ASSAULT GROUP

parachutes and diving. On January 19th, 1979, the first course concluded and Their Majesties the King and Queen of Spain attended the closing ceremonies. On February 23rd, the Unit was presented to the media, just before the second course began, attended by another 50 or so police officers.

During the consolidation process, Captain García-Quijada, the GEO's first director, died in an automobile accident and was substituted by Captain Senso, who would also lose his life in May of 1980, while escorting General Sáenz de Santamaría, the Government's special delegate for Security in the Basque Provinces. In its two decades of existence, the GEO members have participated in various, especially complex operations, including: the freeing of Doctor Iglesias Puga and the industry head Guzmán Uribe, abducted by terrorists, as well as the girl Melodie Nackachian, abducted by an organized crime group; the capture of ten armed robbers holding more than two hundred people hostage at the headquarters of the Banco Central in Barcelona; the rescue of hostages held captive at a Bilbao office of the Banco de Vizcaya in 1981, and of others at a Barcelona office of the Banco de Sabadell in 1986. GEO members freed hostages in different prisons as well, with the operations carried out in 1983 and 1985 at the prison in Carabanchel and in 1987 at the Basauri Prison standing out for their brilliance. They also participated as special security forces for the Middle East Peace Summit, the Olympic Games in Barcelona and visits to Spain of such VIPs as His Holiness the Pope and successive US presidents. They were present as well in the last two airplane hijackings occurring in Spain –in both cases, the hijackers surrendered due to the intervention of Police negotiators trained and coordinated by the GEO.

One of its most significant activities has been the fight against terrorist groups, especially against the radical Basque organization, ETA, a mission which it has been carrying out from 1980 to the present. During this time, it has captured approximately two hundred commando members in operations requiring apartment raids or high risk detentions. The GEO has dismantled a total of over thirty armed terrorist commandos, including, among those belonging to ETA, the commandos Madrid, Barcelona, Goyerri-Costa, Matalaz, Donosti, Txirrita, Iñaqui Quijera,

Andutx, Pagaza, Andraitz, Irati, Xira, Gorbea, and many others. Particularly significant was the operation launched in 1995 to capture three ETA terrorists who planned on firing against the King of Spain, Juan Carlos I.

The Comandos Autónomos Anticapitalistas (CAA), the Exercito Guerrillheiro do Povo Galego Ceive (EGPGC) and the Grupo Revolucionario Anticapitalista Primero

AN/AVS-9 NIGHT VISION GLASSES

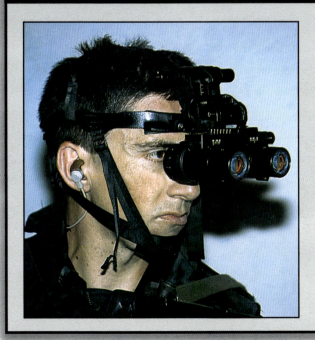

This is an optronic light-intensifying module, manufactured by the US company ITT Defense & Electronics under code number F4949. It is built into the front of a brace that can be attached to the user's head by means of adjustable straps. In the front is the vision element, with two 3rd generation intensifier tubes, born as a result of the US Omnibus IV Program, supported by a completely adjustable module allowing ergonomic adaptation to the face.

When activated, it notably amplifies residual light, the field of vision is 40 degrees, minimum resolution is 1.00 cy/mr, it has a vertical adjustment range of 25 millimeters and interpupillary adjustment ranges from 52 to 72 mm. The binoculars weigh 540 grams, the entire module weighing 790, and has a life of 35 hours when using two 1.5 volt alkaline batteries. Operational temperature ranges from –32º C to 52º C. Its light intensifying elements are designed to close automatically if an intense ray of light crosses their path to prevent blinding the user.

GEO: SPANISH POLICE CORPS ASSAULT GROUP

Barracks
This is the central building of the Guadalajara barracks where the GEO headquarters are located. Designed many years ago for other uses, it has been adapted for its present function; nonetheless, the GEO officers need better facilities to allow for a higher level of training and availability.

de Octubre (GRAPO) have also been its target on repeated occasions.

Other activities entrusted to the GEO have required their operative teams to work temporarily abroad, providing security to Spanish diplomatic delegations at times of danger in countries such as Algeria, Cuba, Iraq, Lebanon, Liberia and Zaire, or detaining especially dangerous criminals and members of clans such as the Turkish Mafia or the Camorra of Naples, French armed robbers and numerous organized groups consisting of South American criminals and immigrants from Eastern Europe. Recently, the GEO has conducted spectacular raid operations on ships at sea as part of the fight against large scale drug trafficking. In the last few months, it has had significant success, capturing the Miami Express and the Tamsaare in two separate operations in the Atlantic and seizing a total of more than twelve tons of cocaine that were to be introduced into Europe through Spain.

Long and complex training

To date, more than four hundred officers have already joined this highly prestigious Unit, after having undergone a "methodical, rational, progressive and reiterative" training program, in the words of a former director. Depending on the vacancies available and more or less biannually, a notice is published in the Orden General, an official government publication, calling candidates to apply for the "Specialization Course for Admission to GEO". Candidates may include civil servants at the basic level and occasionally inspectors as well.

After the applications have been received, the pre-selection process begins, in which various aspects are considered, such as whether the candidates have martial arts training or know how to deactivate explosives. The best candidates go on to the selection stage, which includes a medical examination, physical tests and decision-making tests, so as to reduce the group to a select number who then attend technical-professional tests and psycho-technological tests, ending this stage with several days of living together, during which the appropriateness of the selected candidates is confirmed. These are usually approximately 10 % of the original number of applicants.

The course, passed by approximately 50 % of those who start it, lasts seven months, spent in barracks. It takes place in the Guadalajara headquarters, is progressive and its professors are principally members of GEO themselves. The course includes both theoretical classes and the most varied of practical training in the fields of police science and technology, instruments, legal matters and socio-

Aiming
The submachine guns and assault rifles used by GEO officers are equipped with mechanisms to aid in aiming, including sights such as this Holosight, with a flat viewing screen and a red dot to serve as a reference point for aiming.

GEO: SPANISH POLICE CORPS ASSAULT GROUP

professional aspects.

Operative action techniques, evasive driving, visual inspection, tailing and surveillance, shooting, handling and activating explosives, helicopter activities, procedural law, tai-jitsu and personal police defense, swimming skills and a base in human psychology constitute some of the subjects studied, with the object of training the students physically as well as preparing them in general for carrying out the activities entrusted. Examinations are constantly given to verify students' achievements and their level of integration in the group.

Once this initial training period has been completed and depending on the vacancies, the trainees go on to enter the Operative Groups, where they work with more experienced partners, gradually gaining confidence in carrying out the different activities. With time, they can improve their potential through more complex training and workshops such as (underwater) assault diving, ship's captain, security driving, shooting instructor or physical education instructor.

Precision
GEO snipers have a wide range of rifle models, among which are the Heckler und Koch PSG-1D semiautomatic rifles, a weapon of notable precision that stands out for its impeccable operation and its long polygonal barrel.

Reaction
When GEO police officers are assigned to escort VIPs visiting Spain, they do so with motorcades prepared to react against anyone attempting to assassinate the person under protection.

Other significant aspects of their preparation as a group are the activities scheduled with foreign units to gain skills and share experience, both bilaterally and in joint meetings, as well as in international competitions. The GEO usually participates in the traditional competitions periodically organized by the German Grenzschutzgruppe 9 (GSG-9) at their base in St. Augustin (Germany), where units from the world over come together to compete in operative activities combining physical, tactical and shooting aspects. Indeed, at the last competition, in which more than forty groups participated, the GEO team once again placed Spain among the highest ranks, as it was only beaten by the Swiss and the German teams in the overall score.

GEO: SPANISH POLICE CORPS ASSAULT GROUP

Movement
The Spanish special police officers are skilled in moving freely in the most varied scenarios. They have thus mastered rappelling techniques that allow them to reach the most ideal places for carrying out the assigned missions.

Functional organization
The Unit is divided into an Operative Division and a Support Division, both having a total of approximately one hundred and eighty officers. The former has three Operative Action Groups (Grupos de Acción Operativa, or GAO), identified as 10, 20 and 30, commanded by a chief inspector or an inspector, with two Operative Subgroups, led by sub-inspectors and each composed of three Operative Commandos of five officers each, of which two are snipers using long-barreled firearms, one is a specialist in locks and explosives, another is in charge of handling the special systems given him, and the fifth is a frogman.

These scuba diving specialists, who have trained both with the Navy and the Army, constitute the Diving Group. Their principle mission is underwater search and location, using the specific means assigned them. They carry out exercises and training in the nearest swamps and rivers. This unit takes action in specific missions, such as recovering objects thrown into the water by criminals, or reconnaissance of the sea bottom in case of special events.

There is also a constant exchange of personnel with foreign groups, such as Britain's Special Air Service (SAS), Austria's Gendarmerie EinsatzKommando (GEK) Cobra, the Italian Carabinieri's Gruppo Intervento Speciale (GIS), the Italian State Police Force's Nucleo Operativo Centrale di Sicurezza (NOCS), Belgium's Scadron Spécial d'Intervention (ESI) and Portugal's Grupo de Operaçoes Especiais (GOE), among the most significant.

GEO members have also served as special instructors for: the Guinean President Obiang Nguema's personal guards; Ecuador's Escuadrón Especial (EEE), belonging to the Special Forces Brigade (Brigada de Fuerzas Especiales, BFE), which has now adopted the name of Grupo Especial de Operaciones (GEO) of Ecuador; Honduras' Grupo Especial de Operaciones (GEO); Algeria's Group d'Intervention Spécial (GIS); and other special units in Mexico and Egypt.

The most operative
The GEO constitutes a very special unit that is organically and functionally subject to the Police Deputy Director of Operations. Its head is a commissioner who directs the operations of the specialized units, that are supported by other police officers in charge of technical, maintenance or security support at the Guadalajara base.

GEO: SPANISH POLICE CORPS ASSAULT GROUP

Also included in the Operative Division is the Operative Group for Training and Specialization (Grupo Operativo de Formación y Especialidades), constituting the core of course instructors and supported by the activities of the GAO, as well as an Operative Group for Techniques and Testing (Grupo Operativo de Técnicas y Experiencias), in charge of testing all methods it deems necessary, and conducting studies regarding the diverse objectives that could be the targets of terrorist action.

The Support Group includes fifty or so officers who collaborate with the Operative Division. It is divided into the Administrative and Health Support Group, the Technical Automotive Group, in charge of vehicle maintenance, the Technical Means Administration Group, supervising diverse maintenance tasks for armament and communications material, and a Security Subgroup in charge of surveillance of the premises serving as Base for the Unit.

This organization occupies a barracks near the city of Guadalajara, on ample

Aircraft
The Barajas Airport, on the outskirts of Madrid, is a large airport facility where GEO officers train in assaulting a wide variety of aircraft, a technique requiring a great deal of rapport among the people participating in the operation.

grounds with various training areas, including a pool for swimming exercises, a track, a small building to practice entering apartments using explosives, and firing ranges of up to 50 meters; a heliport for helicopters of the General Police Authorities and other larger ones; hangars for vehicle and boat storage; and a main building of several stories with shooting galleries, offices, maintenance workshops, storage rooms, a magazine, stores, gymnasiums, training apartments, planning rooms, lodgings and other facilities necessary for the GEO's daily functioning. In addition, one of the façades of the building is used as a scaling wall to practice rock climbing and the rest of the building is used for practicing rappel.

This special unit has seven basic functions assigned to it, covering a wide range of possibilities: freeing persons who have been abducted or taken hostage; capturing or neutralizing members of terrorist groups and dangerous armed criminals, whether based in the country or coming from abroad; opening doors and

Teamwork
During assaults, the officers usually advanced in a group, covering possible reactions against them. In this manner, they are sure to reach the point where their operation is to commence without having been detected.

GEO: SPANISH POLICE CORPS ASSAULT GROUP

EDS LASER TRANSMITTER

To facilitate aim with MP5 submachine guns, by daylight or by night, a dual system has been acquired from the US company, Electronic Defense and Security, consisting of a group of three lasers in a very small module of anodized aluminum that can be affixed to the small hole provided for cleaning at the muzzle.

This element, powered by a rechargeable battery in the weapon's handguard, includes a pre-selector for the laser unit, an activator button and the three laser-diode components. One of them operates at a wavelength of 630 nanometers and allows aiming during the daytime, including under bright light, while the other two work together, with a sight and a light that operate at 830 nanometers –the infrared light spectrum- requiring night vision glasses and allowing the target to be viewed even in total darkness.

The useful life of the laser-diode is approximately 10,000 hours, with the aiming system weighing 85 grams excluding the handguard. The buttons are resistant to grease and dirt, and the lighting module is affixed with an Allen wrench.

entering premises where there are members of terrorist or organized crime groups using special techniques; participation in special protective contingents; providing security services at diplomatic headquarters and consulates of Spain abroad in situations of danger; carrying out underwater reconnaissance in search of victims, explosive devices or any other effects associated with the commission of a crime; and in general, carrying out any police service requiring special training.

Modern armaments

GEO officers wear black outfits during training and assault missions, very flexible black combat boots, facemasks for security reasons, Bolle safety glasses, Draguër gas masks, bulletproof vests with pockets for communication devices and secondary weapons, and a new-generation bulletproof helmet. These elements are complemented by a tactical jacket and leggings specially designed for boat raid operations.

Their weapons are also highly advanced and, as a basic element, include the German Heckler und Köch (H&K) MP5 submachine gun in its compact version K, its normal version with rigid or folding buttstock, and the silenced version, SD. All of them are chambered for the 9x19 millimeter Parabellum cartridge and have integrated rear optical or optronic sights on the body, Sure-Fire flashlights on the handguard and visible or infrared lasers at the front. As secondary weapons, both Manurhin MR-73, .38 Special / .357 Magnum revolvers and P-9S pistols for 9 mm Parabellum can be used. The latter are being substituted by Sig Sauer P-226 steel pistols with optional laser sights and built-in flashlights.

For operations requiring other types of weapons, 12 caliber shotguns can be used, models H&K 512, Franchi 230 and SPS 350, as well as Remington "Wingmaster", the first of which is semiautomatic and the rest manually operated. They also use various models of 5.56x45 mm caliber rifles (.223 Remington), including H&K 33E, 33 KE, 53 and G41, and Sig Sauer models 551 SWAT and 552 Commando, weapons which can be fitted with optronic sights aiding firing in situations requiring speed and instinct.

In operations requiring maximum precision, highly sophisticated rifles are used, equipped with semiautomatic functions or bolt-operated* manual reloading. Among the former are H&K PSG-1 D, 33 SG/1 and G3 FS, while the latter include the Mauser 66 SP, Sig Sauer SSG-2000, Sako TRG-21 and Sako A2 in a version with integrated silenced barrel, all of them of 7.62x51 caliber. In addition, the Sako TRG-41, .338 Lapua Magnum allows targets to be reached at distances greater than 1,000 meters. On the front, day vision sights such as Zeiss Diavari, Schmidt & Bender or Hensdoltz are ins-

GEO: SPANISH POLICE CORPS ASSAULT GROUP

talled, or night vision sights such as Varo AN/PVS-4 or Simrad KN-250F.

Sophisticated equipment
The activities of the GEO as a special police unit require the use of highly sophisticated material in very specific fields. For this reason, GEO officers use such scuba diving equipment as neoprene wetsuits, diving knives, life vests, dry suits for immersion in cold waters, underwater compasses, manometers to verify pressure, 18-liter, single compressed air bottles and 22-liter dual compressed air bottles, weighted belts, goggles, regulators, Aladin diving computers, underwater flashlights, special communications equipment, underwater robots and cameras, rubber dinghies of various

Compact
The MP5K is a very compact submachine gun that can be hidden under a jacket or in a briefcase. Its firing capacity is impressive, as it fires 9x19 millimeter Parabellum cartridges at a rhythm of nearly a million per minute.

Equipment
In the course of 1999, GEO officers have received different types of additional equipment, including new helmets, tactical combat vests, leg holsters for the new pistol and the 5.56x45 caliber SIG assault rifle.

types facilitating surface travel, and underwater propulsion jets able to propel two people underwater so as to significantly reduce their effort in reaching the specific location where a task must be carried out.

For entrance to closed premises, GEOs can use various instruments, including jimmies, sledge hammers, diverse types of explosives, portable cutting equipment such as portable heat torches and pliers that allow fences to be cut easily. For use immediately after entering, if the situation calls for it, are Falken F505 stun grenades that combine detonations with intense flares of light to prevent the reaction of those within the premises. For movement through particularly steep areas or to reach difficult locations, they can use dynamic and static

ropes, as well as various types of ladders and poles.

They also have other special material on hand, including laser measuring devices to measure the exact distance to the target; spotlights to illuminate specific areas and facilitate teamwork; control panels that permit coordination of sni-

GEO: SPANISH POLICE CORPS ASSAULT GROUP

Kilometer range
The Finnish precision rifle Sako TRG-41 fires .338 caliber Lapua Magnum ammunition, designed for great precision at distances of over one kilometer, a very useful range in a variety of police operation scenarios.

pers; Zodiac Hurricane semi-rigid dinghies, used for assault on boats and propelled by two powerful outboard Yamaha motors with 130 horsepower each, providing high speed to prevent the assaulted boat's crew from reacting; and nocturnal vision devices, including Philips BM8028A1 binocular glasses with 2nd generation image intensifier tubes, the modern ITT AN/AVS-9 with 3rd generation tubes, and ITT Pocketscope F6010 night sight, with 4th generation "Ultra Tube" tubes, equipped with infrared lighting for vision in places with total absence of light.

Also special is the communication equipment used to maintain contact among commando members or between GEO group leaders and superior echelons. Among this equipment are the US Motorola MX-340, MX-350, MX-1000 and MX-2000, and portable VHF and HF relay stations. Some of this equipment has encrypted emission to avoid interference by non-authorized tapping means, while other equipment is specially protected for any possible immersion in water that may become necessary during marine missions.

Frogmen
The GEO includes a diver unit specializing in carrying out the most varied of missions underwater, whether on the coast or in fresh water. They are normally trained in rivers, swamps and the sea.

GEO: SPANISH POLICE CORPS ASSAULT SQUAD

The quick arrival of GEO forces to the scene of action can be the key to their success. They therefore use the Police's MBB BO-105 light helicopters, from which they can, for example, carry out command tasks or locate snipers, passenger transport aircraft when necessary, and their own vehicles stored in underground parking lots at the Guadalajara base.

The latter include high-cylinder, camouflaged automobiles normally manned by four people, vans for materials transport, specially designed trailers for diving equipment and support material, specially designed mobile homes that are used as mobile command centers, semi trucks for transporting specific equipment and armored cars used in high risk areas. They also use vans specially equipped for transport of explosives, ambulances and coaches for quick transport of especially relevant units.

Furthermore, they are also assigned off-road motorcycles, Yamaha XJ 900 S and BMW K100 road motorcycles for high-speed operations, Mercedes 280G

Shooting galleries
At the Guadalajara headquarters there are several shooting galleries on the lower floors, used to program the most varied training for the officers, who use personal weapons there against all sorts of targets.

and Toyota Land Cruiser off-road vehicles for driving through rough terrain, and Nissan Patrol off-road vehicles, adapted so that an assault ladder can be placed on the roof for rapid access to high areas, such as the hatches of passenger transport aircraft.

The efficiency of the GEO has been sufficiently demonstrated, as it has succeeded in all the missions entrusted it since its creation. The excellent results achieved and the enormous variety of activities it carries out makes the GEO a truly valuable special operations group.

Personal defense
All GEO members have mastered various martial arts techniques to handle various police situations without having to resort to weapons. These techniques are practiced assiduously in the Unit's gymnasium.

PERSONAL PROTECTIVE GEAR

The missions assigned to police assault groups, in which the officers must often face extremely well-armed criminals, involve an elevated risk for assault team members of being hit by enemy fire. This high risk, along with the need to carry out dynamic team operations in a coordinated manner with the participation of all the police forces, has lead to the adoption of a series of personal security measures, consisting of training to make officers skilled in executing their movements with great speed and precision, such that the opponent does not have time to react; and in equipping the officers with personal protective gear, generally bullet-proof vests and helmets, whose function is to stop or reduce the effects of the weapons used against their police action.

Generalized use

There are many manufacturers whose principal activity is the design and production of advanced fibers and light materials that can be used for personal protective gear and, as a complement, for protection of vehicles. In great part

A firm fit
Bulletproof helmets are normally adjusted on the head by means of a strap with chin-piece, such that when the police officer runs or moves, it remains in the optimal position to fulfill its protective function.

Safety
Police assault squads are exposed to high risk situations in which they may be hit by bullets from weapons fired by terrorists or criminals. Therefore they conduct operations wearing all sorts of protective gear.

implemented in the United States and Europe, their representatives promote their products throughout the world, offering them at the most prestigious of fairs and exhibits. It is excellent publicity for a company if its products are chosen by a reputed police squad –this will help them to obtain new sales contracts in the future.

All of these manufacturers make efforts to proclaim, through well-planned publicity extolling the virtues of their products, that their articles are different because they weigh less, are efficient in withstanding impacts, are more comfortable or less expensive, aspects which, among a great many others, could make the customer choose one brand over another.

PERSONAL PROTECTIVE GEAR

Advanced materials

In the 80s, products became available made of revolutionary new materials such as Kevlar, that are lightweight and highly resistant, often stronger than steel in a strength/weight ratio, and they are at the same time ductile, allowing them to be adapted to shapes and sizes according to the function they are to execute.

After evaluating various options that have included, for example, the manufacture of bulletproof helmets in titanium or tungsten, a new revolution has occurred and even lighter and tougher materials have appeared, but much more expensive than the previous ones and than ceramic ones, which are still half as expensive as aramidas fibers. Among the most commonly used are Spectrashield Plus, Goldflex, Quadralink, Kevlar –especially in its new versions designated with the addition of a 29–, Comfort NFT (New Fiber Technology) and UHMWPE (Unidirectional Polyethyl Polyethylene), Nylon 6.6 (Poly-Hexamethylene Diamine Adipate) or Twaron by Akzo Nobel, which is five times more resistant than steel.

They all have significant features, such as resistance to humidity or friction, elasticity, flexibility, etc., characteristics which help define their capacity to withstand impacts. These characteristics can be evaluated according to the various norms applied in different countries, among the most well-known of which are: the United States NIJ (National Institute of Justice) with norms such as 0108.1 or 0101.03, the Dutch Council and TNO, the German Technische Richtlinie Schutzwesten and Mellrichstadt, the Belgian BEAF, the British PSDB or the Asi-Rab of Arabic countries, while the companies comply with ISO quality norms 9001 and 9002. They can also comply with various of NATO's STANAG, such as 2920, which measures the capacity for stopping 1.1 gram shrapnel.

German equipment
The GSG-9 and the SEK are some of the police equipment made in Germany, a country which has pioneered in preparing special police forces. For this reason, their protective gear is also among the vanguard.

Vital areas
This SWAT officer from Mesa is wearing a bullet-proof vest with pelvic protection and a thick helmet on his head, elements which protect the majority of his vital areas from possible impacts.

Level of protection

Basically, the rating of personal protective gear is done on a scale that defines the level of protection (i.e. capacity to withstand impacts) that each product provides, based on the elements used in their manufacture and the thickness of the material. The lowest rating is Level I, covering those products, generally lighter, that are shrapnel-proof –i.e., they are capable of withstanding the shrapnel produced in grenade explosions or other

15

PERSONAL PROTECTIVE GEAR

High risk
The head is the area of the body where it is most dangerous to receive the impact of a bullet. That is why manufacturers design all sorts of helmets, some even having an armored screen in the front facilitating vision and protecting the face.

devices that generate shrapnel - and they are strong enough to protect the user from: .22 Long Rifle cartridges loaded with 40- grain tips fired at a speed of 320 meters per second; .25 Auto loaded with 50 g bullets with metallic blankets at 247 m/s; and .38 Special with 158 g semiwadcuter bullets at 259 m/s.

The next level is IIA, covering materials capable of stopping such ammunition as .22 Magnum, 125 g .38 Spl. + P SJHP travelling at 314 m/s, or 158 g JHP at 377 m/s, 230 g armored .45 ACP at 247 m/s, .357 Magnum with 158 g semiwadcuter bullets fired at 382 m/s, 170 g .10 mm Auto JHP at 357 m/s and 9x19 millimeter Parabellum both with 100 g JHP bullets at 381 m/s and 115 g tips at 354 m/s. Level II gear is the most commonly used by police assault squadrons due to its technical qualities of withstanding ammunition such as .44 Magnum with 250 g bullets at 427 m/s or 9mm Finnish Lapua fired with a submachine gun at a velocity of 427 m/s. There are also vests rated at Level IIIA.

Maximum security in protective gear is achieved by inserting sheets in special front and back pockets on the vest, made of advanced fibers or ceramic composites at Levels III and IV, designed to withstand impacts from all types of rifles and assault guns, those in the former category being capable of withstanding the effects of cartridges such as the Soviet 7.62x39mm or the 7.62x51 mm standardized by the North Atlantic Treaty Organization (NATO); while those in the latter can even stop perforating ammunition such as 30.06 loaded with 166 g bullets reaching impact at 868 m/s.

Sometimes very economic metallic sheets are also inserted for use in concrete situations.

Rapid response
The members of special squads within police corps are trained and equipped to respond rapidly to any incident that may occur. Hence, they always take their bulletproof vests and helmets with them.

PERSONAL PROTECTIVE GEAR

BULLET-PROOF VESTS

The police officers assigned to special assault units use diverse protective elements to cover vulnerable areas of the body. The torso has always been an area of the body with various organs which must be protected from perforation produced by impacts from rounds fired by adversaries, so that various types of bullet-proof vests are needed, which are becoming increasingly light and more comfortable.
Vest can be designed for use under clothing –as in the illustration–, used for covert operations or operations carried out in plain clothes, or for use over clothing, for operations that don't need special secrecy. These garments are usually held in place on the torso by Velcro-type, self-adhesive straps or other elements such as zippers or adjustment straps. Correctly placed and depending on their level of protection, they are enough to detain bullet impacts and stop attacks with daggers or other cutting weapons. The officer can nonetheless, suffer hematomas or broken bones as a result of the concentrated discharge of kinetic energy received at the specific point of impact of a bullet.

Wide range

Many officers' lives have been saved though the use of personal protective gear during police operations. There are even associations of officers who, using products of a specific brand, have survived armed confrontation in which they were reached by enemy fire. These companies are present and available in the majority of Western and Asiatic countries, and in many cases, their products are manufactured with materials made by the most renowned firms. They advertise their products in a variety of media and use the most varied sales strategies –including criticizing their competitors- to close contracts.

Personal protection

The United States and Germany are leaders in the sector, with Great Britain also in a good position. In the United States in this specific market, such companies as American Body Armor offer their Tactical Armor Vest 2, rated at Level IIA, protecting against impacts from 9mm fired with submachine guns, Gentex International sells several helmets, specializing in casting protective cups in Kevlar, Point Blank Body Armor, in collaboration with SWAT in Los Angeles, has designed the Modular Response Vest range, Pro-Tec Armored Products offers

PERSONAL PROTECTIVE GEAR

Tactical Vests, there are various products by Second Chance Body Armor, and new designs by Safariland, meeting the most demanding requirements.

In Germany, companies such as Mehler Vario System are outstanding. In Great Britain, Dowty Armourshield's General Purpose Vest has been successful, and Highmark Manufacturing products in Belfast, whereas in France, some noteworthy firms are Confection Sèvre Vendée de Cerizay. Some noteworthy products by other firms are the MASKA-1 helmet by the Russian company Research Institute of Special Technics, which offers head and face protection against 9mm bullet impacts, tactical combat vests by the Czech firm Petris Solnice, or the latest bullet-proof helmets that the Spanish company Fedur has designed for the Spanish Police Corps' Special Operations Group (Grupo Especial de Operaciones, or GEO).

Protection en route

Some assault squads are assigned various types of armored shields as well, which, depending on their level, are capable of stopping all sorts of bullets and shrapnel produced by the explosion of a grenade thrown at them. Some are small, measuring 60x50 centimeters, and are often used by the leaders of dynamic assault operations. There are also shields that are double the size. There are even heavy shields on the market that require wheels to be moved to the deployment area.

Bomb protection
Some police assault squads throughout the world include explosives experts capable of carrying out explosive deactivation missions, and who are also in charge of placing explosives to facilitate officer entrance into buildings. When on duty, they wear thick, heavy bombproof suits.

Among the offers proposed by diverse manufacturers –which feature as well small armored windows on the upper part so as to keep what is occurring in view, or have lights affixed to the sides– are the Ballistic Protective Shields (BPS), manufactured in composite materials by the British firm Dowty Armourshield, equipped with an element that reduces the shock of impact to the arm of the officer holding it, or products by the Israeli company Phasan Sasa, that offers two models made of hybrid composite materials with high detainment capacity.

Pro-tec, subsidiary of the Armor Holdings group, one of the principal manufacturers in the world, offers a wide range that

Shield
There are a variety of models of armor-plated shields on the market to protect officers during their advance. Although they are heavy, they give a high level of protection in case the criminals are well armed and open fire on the police officers.

PERSONAL PROTECTIVE GEAR

Personal gear
Police officers, such as this one from the SWAT team in Atlanta, usually equip themselves in their vehicles before commencing an operation or training. Protective gear –like this thick, dark-colored vest standing out over the uniform– is the first thing they put on.

includes models such as the small Patroller, weighing 3.9 kg and measuring 45x60 cm; the medium-sized Defender, weighing 7.2 kg and measuring 50x85, that can be optimized with an outer illumination set and includes a sight; Entry Two, weighing 10.8 kg and measuring 60x120 cm; Nato 3, weighing 36.5 kg, that can be moved on an inner set of 3 wheels; and the Phoenix IV, weighing 71.2 kg, with an additional 29.3 if equipped with the optional armored sight, and requiring four wheels to move it with comfort. The former three offer IIA protection level, the fourth product is Level III and the fifth Level IV.

Great capacity
In operations where there is reason to believe that the adversary may be armed with very powerful rifles, it can be very useful to have ceramic sheets, such as this one that a Texan SWAT agent is displaying. They are capable of stopping high-caliber bullets.

Also from the United States are such manufacturers as American Body Armor in Florida, that offers TAC-500R shields made of a sheet of Kevlar and outstanding for their weight of only 12.7 kilograms despite their height of 876 millimeters and width of 533; Safariland in Ontario, California, with a catalogue that includes a line of three different models, and Pro-Tec Armored Products in Pittsfield, Massachusetts, manufacturing no less than 14 different models combining Spectra Shield with ceramic materials.

NOCS: ITALIAN SPECIAL POLICE

Italy is a country severely affected by the criminal activity of its Mafia clans, by the action of various terrorist groups active in the past, and by the power of attraction that its powerful industry has on high-level international criminals. To guarantee the resolution of situations that require the intervention of more prepared groups than regular police officers, the Italian Police Corps has established a special assault squad consisting of tough men with many years of hard training and experience. This squad is called the Central Operative Group for Security (Nùcleo Operativo Centrale di Sicurezza, or NOCS)..

An evident need

As had occurred in Germany in 1972, when the Israeli sports delegation attending the Olympic Games was attacked by terrorists from the Black September organization, the Italians also had an incident which changed everything, defining a "before" and an "after" in their capacity to handle high risk police situations: the attack on the Fiumicino Airport in Rome in 1974.

Parachuting
Skydiving with manually operated parachutes, a technique well known by a good deal of the personnel of this Italian police group, allows the officers to reach the ground with precision and secrecy.

Process of creation

The results of the attack mentioned above, and especially the deficiencies that it made evident, lead the Ispettorato Generale per l'Azione contro il Terrorismo (General Inspector for Action Against Terrorism) to push for the creation of a squadron specially trained to handle this type of threats. This Division was transformed into the Servizio Di Sicurezza (SDS) the next year. In May of 1975, said squadron was ready. It was called the Nùcleo Anticomando, whose leadership was given to Andrea Scandurra, who had significant experience as he had been a member of the Scuadriglie Antibanditismo deployed towards the end of the sixties in Sardinia and Calabria to deal with the Mafia that inhabit these regions of Italy. Scandurra's men began to train, especially in the physical aspect and in handling equipment, in order to take action and capture terrorists, preventing armed conflict that could endanger possible victims.

To achieve this, they adopted methods

NOCS: ITALIAN SPECIAL POLICE

Scuba diving specialists
Canguro 420 rubber dinghies, powered by outboard motors, are used by specialists for activities carried out on the water. Noteworthy are the camouflage neoprene suits that the police officers are wearing.

based on surprise and speed, which proved highly successful during their first operations against members of the Nuclei Armati Proletari (NAP) and the extreme right-wing groups of the Ordine Nuovo. The results obtained encouraged them to continue training in other areas as well, such as handling explosives or using precision weapons, a process which allowed them to improve their general skill over a short period. It was done while they continued deployment in high risk areas to execute more operative actions.

The first great change in the Núcleo Anticomando was caused by the Minister of the Interior, Francesco Cossiga, who promoted the enactment of a new law, dated October 24th, 1977, establishing operative units for antiterrorist activities and special operations. This led to a profound reorganization of the Italian intelligence and security institutions in 1978.

As a result of all of this, the Nùcleo Operativo Centrale di Sicurezza was born, and the unit has maintained this name to the present. From then on, NOCS officers, under the command of

Assault vehicles
NOCS members use Mitsubishi vehicles for their operations which are specially modified with lateral supports and reinforcement bars on the roof, allowing for rapid transport in total security for a group of six officers to the point where they must carry out their mission.

NOCS: ITALIAN SPECIAL POLICE

the director of the 4th División del Ufficio Centrale Investigazioni Generali e Operazioni Speciali (UCIGOS), began a very active period during which they carried out many satisfactory operations against members of organizations such as the Red Brigades, the Armed Revolutionary Group or First Line, operations that led to more than one hundred arrests, including such terrorists as Giovanni Schiavone, Viscardi, Susanna Ronconi and Settepani.

Freeing General Dozier

At the beginning of 1982, a very significant incident occurred that was to change everything in the history of this Italian police group: the Red Brigades abducted US General James L. Dozier. After a lengthy search, the place where he was being held was located. It was a house in Padua, and it was decided to send in a NOCS assault squad to free him. This operation was carried out with great success and gained widespread international renown as it occupied the cover story of newspapers and television news programs.

Paratrooper
This NOCS officer is diving from an Agusta Bell helicopter belonging to the Italian Police Corps with a manually opening parachute, and arrives covertly at the precise landing point.

Total silence
An officer, armed with a German MP5SD submachine gun equipped with built-in silencer, crouches among the foliage in the woods awaiting the order to fire. From this position, he can reach a target at a distance of 100 meters with total precision.

As a consequence of such a successful operation (the abductors were armed with approximately ten Model 34 Beretta pistols equipped with silencers) the General himself sent a letter, dated June 23rd of the same year and written in Italian, to Colonel Maurizio Genolini of the Italian Police, in which he thanked him for the efficiency and high level of professionalism demonstrated in the assault. To reward them for their excellent action, the Texan oil magnate Ross Perot gave them twelve Smith & Wesson pistols, of 7.65 millimeter caliber, with a special engraving on the slide: "For the rescue of brigadier general Dozier", for the group of officers who participated in that mission.

In 1983, there was another reorganization of the Italian Police Forces, and the UCIGOS rose to the level of Directing Organization, changing its initials to DCPP (Direzione Centrale Polizia di Prevenzione), which are still used to date. From that year until 1986, small organizational changes were introduced into the NOCS to adapt it to the country's internal situation and that led to the expansion of its mission to include VIP protection and support for the Uffici Anticrimine.

In 1989, they participated in a night operation against criminals who had abducted the industry businessman Dante Beladinelli, an operation in which the Lancia Delta vehicle that the captors were using was hit by copious gunfire in the windshield and the sides as a result of the shootings between the captors and the police. At the beginning of the 90s, they carried out various significant operations: in 1990 they began collaborating

NOCS: ITALIAN SPECIAL POLICE

PARATROOPERS

Only some of the world's police assault squads have paratroopers in their groups, as this technique is more appropriate to military needs than those of the police. Nonetheless, Italian police officers who are members of the Nùcleo Operativo Centrale de Sicurezza are trained in skydiving using automatic parachutes, allowing them to dive from various types of large transport airplanes and helicopters.

Skydiving with manual parachutes is a more complex technique, requiring a longer preparation and the use of another type of parachute which provides greater precision. With these, police officers can reach the exact point from which to start their police action, or allow for a great distance between the initial diving and final landing points. They also allow for diving from small aircraft such as the Italian Police Corps' AB-412 helicopters.

with Criminalpol to handle organized crime groups; in 1991 they took action to help in the liberation of Kuwait by an international force and to prevent terrorist acts promoted by Iraq, and in the same year also participated in the freeing of the boy Augusto de Megni, who had been abducted; in 1994 they freed 134 hostages who had been held in an airplane on a runway of the Fiumicino Airport in Rome; after the assassination of the judges Falcone and Borsellino, they were assigned for the first time as personal protection unit for the Attorney General of Italy in Palermo. At present, the group continues to carry out tasks associated with the detention of criminals, terrorists or anyone putting the security of the State at jeopardy.

In said activities, following the motto "Sicut Nox Silentes", they continue to act as the Divisione Operazioni Speciali of the DCPP and conduct all sorts of missions.

Since they began carrying out their specific tasks, they have participated in approximately five thousand missions, including approximately four hundred security and Judicial Police operations, and about two hundred high risk arrests, that have caused 19 medals of courage to be granted, two wounded in service distinctions, fifty or so merit awards and more than seven hundred honorable mentions. To the previous list of awards must be added 12 silver medals from the United States and various trop-

NOCS: ITALIAN SPECIAL POLICE

Aircraft assault
On the access stairs to an airplane, we can see a group of NOCS officers. Noteworthy are the pistols they are wielding against hypothetical abductors, and their helmets made of Pro-Tec plastic protecting them from blows.

hies obtained in shooting competitions of the International Practical Shooting Confederation (IPSC).

As inevitable consequences of their activity, several officers have been wounded by armed criminals, one of whom became handicapped as a result of his participation in a mission.

Operative participation
There are approximately eighty thousand officers in the Italian Police Corps, under the authority of the Ministry of the Interior, which carries out missions of public security along with the carabinieri and the Guardia di Finanza. The organization of the Ministeri dell'Interno includes the Dipartimento della Pubblica Sicurezza (DPS), under which, in turn, is the Direzione Centrale della Polizia di Prevencione (DCCP), a part of which, through the Divisione Operazioni Speciali (DOS), is the NOCS, a unit consisting of one hundred or so officers.

These officers are supervised by a commander in chief, whom they call "primo dirigente vicequestore", under whose authority is a hierarchy consisting of the Secretariat for Security, whose mission is to fulfill various administrative tasks related to the general paperwork generated by daily work; the Operative Support Division, in charge of maintaining departments that carry out various tasks, from health support to the equipment used by the video and information technology office; and the Operative Division encompassing the police assault groups.

Sophisticated
The equipment assigned this unit includes complex video recording and editing means, used to monitor criminals and to prepare missions and activities in more detail.

NOCS: ITALIAN SPECIAL POLICE

The latter includes two Operative Squadrons for Special Actions, one Operative Security Squadron and the division in charge of monitoring the selection, learning and training processes. Of the first two, one is always ready to take action should an incident occur, and they have at their disposal military aircraft and Police helicopters, with which they can be transported with great speed to the point where they are to carry out a mission. If necessary, the second squadron can take action in few hours to provide the first one with support or replace them if so decided.

These assault squadrons are prepared to carry out a varied range of activities, including: the freeing of hostages with the highest degree of physical security for the hostages as well as the criminals; assault operations in both urban and rural settings for the capture of presumed terrorists and common criminals who there is reason to believe will offer resistance to officers attempting to arrest them; providing support for other Police departments that need a specifically trained group to guarantee the success of their operation; providing support for training in order to select specialized officials; providing temporary high-risk protection for representatives from other countries on official or private visits, as well as for VIPs from Italian institutions, most significantly for members of the Government or judges threatened by the Mafia; and high-risk escorts, both in Italy as well as abroad, where they also carry out activities to protect diplomatic legations.

Protective and escort activities involve establishing an element of coverage very close to the person who is the object of the officers' activity, and the deployment of mobile response units or CATs (Counter Attack Teams) that patrol the vicinity in special vehicles and are strongly armed. Of the long list of VIPs that they have protected, some of the most significant are: the Russian Presidents Mikhail Gorbachov

Real fire
A great deal of the training with firearms done by these is officers is carried out with real fire to get the maximum from their professional qualifications and accustom them to what will happen in real missions.

NOCS: ITALIAN SPECIAL POLICE

and Boris Yeltsin, the King and Queen of Belgium, the Japanese Emperor Akhito and his wife, the Palestine President Arafat and, with the support of the U.S. Secret Service, the United States Presidents Bush and Clinton.

Modern and varied equipment

So that they may carry out their missions, the NOCS agents are equipped with a wide and varied range of weapons, systems and elements which allows them to conduct their activities as a special assault group with greater security. These activities require the perfect combination of highly trained officers and the latest technology in equipment.

Italian and foreign weapons

Proud of the fact that the Italian armaments industry enjoys great international prestige, this unit has acquired various models manufactured in the country, among which are Beretta M92F2 and 8000 Cougar semiautomatic pistols, firing 9x19 millimeter caliber Parabellum ammunition. The former have an accessory on the front of the handguard to mount flashlights with which to light especially dark areas on the premises which are the settings of their assaults. They also have some Tanfoglio pistols of the same caliber, that have been used by their squadron in IPSC Championships.

Also Italian are the Beretta M12, 9 mm-caliber Parabellum submachine guns acquired when the unit was first formed, Franchi 12/70 caliber shotguns, of which they use the SPAS 15 semiautomatic fed with magazines holding six cartridges, and manually operated shotguns that are characterized by their very short barrel and a metallic butt that folds under the body, the Beretta AR70 assault rifles that fire 5.56x45 mm (.223 Remington) ammunition and the AR70/90 ones that are a later model and stand out for their retractable buttstock and the elevated sight base.

Nonetheless, the basic weapon used

PSG-1 PRECISION RIFLE

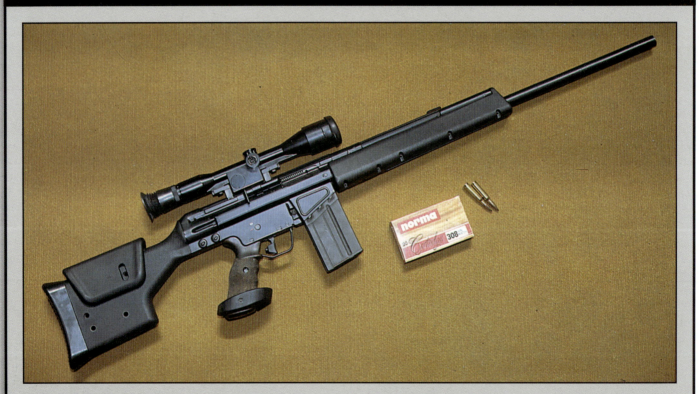

Manufactured by the German company Heckler und Koch, the PSG-1 is considered the most precise 7.62x51-millimeter caliber semiautomatic machine gun in the world. Highly reliable, sufficiently tough for police needs, easy to use and to aim, its only disadvantages are its elevated price and its need for careful maintenance. Equipped with a large, heavy, cold-forged polygonal barrel, it is capable of great precision in reaching targets located at a distance of up to six hundred meters, with the capacity to fire bursts with great speed due to its magazines, with capacity for up to ten cartridges, and the internal mechanisms that eject the empty shells and introduce new cartridges into the chamber. It weighs 8.1 kilograms, measures a total length of 120.8 centimeters, and among its ergonomic qualities are the adjustable slide and butt, ergonomic pistol grip, adjustable trigger and handguard that allows the attachment of a bipod or tripod to give it greater stability.

NOCS: ITALIAN SPECIAL POLICE

Quick travel
The vehicles used by the NOCS allow them to quickly reach the point of departure for their missions. They are also used to carry out secondary missions and in training activities.

in the squadron's deployments is the Heckler und Köch MP5 submachine gun, of which they use the compact A5 and the silenced SD6, weapons firing 9x19 mm ammunition and that can be equipped with flashlights, red dot sights and optical elements such as the Hensoldt Wetzlar with a magnifying power of 4. Other weapons at their disposal are 38 Special /.357 Magnum two-inch revolvers, H&K G41 and Galil SAR assault rifles, both with .223 Remington, and various

7.62x51 mm (.308 Winchester) precision rifles, among which are models such as the German manually-operated Mauser 86 and the semiautomatic H&K G3 SG/1 and PSG-1. To achieve maximum precision, they use optical sights such as Zeiss, with a magnifying power of 6, and nocturnal optronic sights such as the Simrad Optronics KN202.

Special garments and gear

The officers usually wear navy blue body suits or camouflage uniforms very similar to those used by the Italian Army. Accessories include tactical vests that allow partial storage of part of their personal equipment, rigid holsters for short weapons, both for attachment on the leg or at the waist, tactical boots with non-skid soles, facemasks, gloves to protect

Constant training
The tire house is a transformable premises where the Italian special police train. There they simulate assaults with real fire in which they shoot simulated targets with blanks and train in the techniques of movement in reduced spaces.

27

NOCS: ITALIAN SPECIAL POLICE

the hands and accessories such as knives, flashlights and stun grenades.

Protection is provided through an adequate combination of bulletproof vests and helmets, including among the latter a helmet made of Pro-Tec fiber, designed to withstand light blows or impacts, and a bulletproof helmet that stands out for its thick armored visor covering the face. A facial protector made of ceramic materials designed to withstand the impact of light bullets is also used to cover this area.

Transport associated with NOCS deployment is carried out with specially armor-plated vans or in Alfa Romeo cars equipped with high-cylinder engines, whereas in complementary activities, four-wheel-drive Mitsubishis that have been modified to allow their use as assault vehicles may be used, medical evacuation ambulances and four-wheel-drive Mercedes used to transport the trailers carrying the Canguro 420 rubber dinghies. In exceptional cases, or if required, they may use Agusta-Bell 212 helicopters, with capacity for ten or so people, and twin motor Police airplanes from which they can parachute.

This activity requires the equipment that the NOCS has available, consisting of warm outfits to protect against the cold, facial protective goggles, helmets, automatic and manual parachutes, and oxygen equipment allowing them to jump using HAHO (High Altitude, High Opening) and HALO (High Altitude, Low Opening) techniques. In their travel through mountainous areas, backpacks are very useful, as well as rappelling harnesses, ropes of all kinds, and skis and skiing gear. When they carry out activities in the water, they bring neoprene wetsuits to protect themselves against low temperatures, goggles, single compressed air bottles, Technisub closed-circuit oxygen equipment and regulators or hydrostatic vests.

Sharpshooters
NOCS police officers are qualified to use various semiautomatic and bolt-operated precision weapons, and have camouflage uniforms and elements which help them blend into their surroundings to prevent being detected.

Professionals
The members of this Italian special police group are highly motivated officers with a great deal of training who have proven themselves in numerous successfully completed missions.

NOCS: ITALIAN SPECIAL POLICE

Included in the personal gear are EOD 7 armored suits used by explosives experts deactivating bombs and ghillie suit-type camouflage outfits allowing sharpshooters to blend into their surroundings when they are conducting operations in rural settings.

Selection of members

The members of NOCS often train shoulder to shoulder with similar groups from other countries, such as the Hostage Rescue Team (HRT) that the US Federal Bureau of Investigation (FBI) has stationed in Quantico (Virginia), the French National Police Corps' RAID squad, the Spezialeinsatzkommando (SEK) of the Police Corps from the German region of Baden-Wurttemberg or the YA'MA'M of the Israeli National Police Corps. They have even collaborated with the International Long Range Reconnaissance Patrol School (ILRRPS) established in the German town of Weingarten where officers learn reconnaissance techniques in depth, especially small groups selected from among the member countries of the North Atlantic Treaty Organization (NATO).

This is possible because the NOCS members have attained international renown for their personal training, which begins with the selection of their future members from among the personnel of the Polizía di Stato, whose members are nominated by their hierarchical superiors, with the condition that they comply with the requirements of application. One of the first tests they undergo is a personal interview with an active member of the Unit, then they undergo a medical examination, some psychotechnological tests and some athletic tests that include running five kilometers in less than 20 minutes. They also undergo a precision test and a firing test using short weapons and targets located at a range of between 15 and 25 meters.

Depending on the vacancies, the recruits are chosen and they begin initial training lasting six months. Those who are not eliminated from the team continue training through short specialization courses over the course of nearly two more years. This general training as members of assault teams is completed with training in the techniques of scuba diving and skydiving.

They begin acquiring professional experience when they become definitive members of the Operative Squadrons, in which they follow the same program of ongoing training as the rest of their colleagues. This program increases their personal preparation, lends them greater self-confidence and allows their integration into the group such that they gradually take on increasingly complex tasks in settings such as aircraft, train stations and buildings. To complete their training, they travel regularly to the Abbasanta Training Center in Sardinia, a site where they have high rises to practice assaults, buildings for training in maneuvers and even a tire house to practice operations with real fire.

Facial protection
The NOCS is one of the few police assault groups in the world that uses armored face masks, capable of withstanding projectiles fired by small-caliber weapons, saving the life of an officer hit in the face.

Dynamic assault
Three officers of the Italian Police Corps at the entrance to a building awaiting orders to commence an assault mission to be carried out by two of them, while the third one covers the rear to prevent surprise attacks.

COMMUNICATIONS SYSTEMS

For a police assault squad to carry out its varied operations to arrest criminals and terrorists, it requires a very complex program in the areas of selection, training and equipment. The latter is often referred to with regard to the weapons assigned. However, it must be kept in mind that there is certain other equipment without which the success of a mission would be jeopardized, among which communications systems are some of the most vital, as they serve to maintain the contacts necessary to allow communication of information about the adversary, instructions from superior echelons or details relative to the coordination of a mission.

Evident need

These aspects of the program, and many others which we could add to a long list, cause all special police units to have a varied range of equipment, from portable radio-telephones to sophisticated crypto-

graphy devices that encode communications so that they can only be understood by those to whom the message was officially sent. Their interception is nearly impossible –except through the use of complex and very expensive systems that only governmental agencies can afford– by criminals wanting to ascertain police

Worldwide use
The United States firm, Motorola, produces a large part of the police communications equipment used by some of the most important squadrons throughout the world, such as the Spanish Police Corps' special GEO squad.

Placement of the equipment
This agent of the Special Assignments Unit from Phoenix displays how communications equipment is attached. The equipment includes a radio in a back pocket, the wiring connecting to a pectoral activator and to a receiver-transmitter microphone attached to the head.

COMMUNICATIONS SYSTEMS

Varied connections
The many activities carried out by Police Corps special units, both in maintenance work and operations, call for constant contact to achieve improved coordination of their operations.

intentions in order to plan actions to sabotage police missions.

Variety of systems

A great variety of communications must be established on all levels. On the lowest level are communications used by those who constitute the assault group itself and who must be able to maintain contact with their superiors to receive instructions, and with their own partners. All of this must be done, if possible, very automatically and without using the hands, as the officers will be using them to wield personal weapons.

Sensors on the fingertips, sensors on the head under the helmet that receive speech vibrations, neck microphones that transmit movements of the larynx or fixed microphones near the mouth allow them to send their messages, while micro-earphones –generally worn in only one ear, because the other one is left free in order to hear immediate sounds- allow them to hear their colleagues or superiors.

These systems, generally connected by a set of cables affixed with Velcro to tactical combat vests or placed so as to cause the least possible discomfort to the user and are easy to transport, are linked to small radio transmitters placed in the pockets of bulletproof or tactical vests, with a capacity for transmitting within a small radius of action. They can include a security system against interference to prevent attempts at electronic neutralization. Officers also use double or multiple band radios that go from one band to another depending on the circumstances.

At all levels

Also very compact and similar to tho-

Integrated in the vest
This police officer from the US is a Special Weapons and Tactics agent, a group based in Forth Worth, Texas. He is using a communications system equipped with activators and wires that are attached to the combat vest with Velcro to insure that they do not interfere with her movements.

se previously described are the systems used by sharpshooters to receive orders about targets or instructions relative to opening fire, instructions which usually trigger simultaneous fire from two weapons on each of the targets, which insures to a degree of 100 % that the targets will be hit. These teams, which often work from elevated and distant positions from which they dominate the situation and have a wider firing angle, can be coordinated from a firing activation center installed in the cab of a vehicle. It should include a variety of transmission equipment, presentation screens to draw the tactical situation and information reception centers.

The communications systems used by frogmen or paratroopers during their operations are also special. Equipment used by the former is water-resistant, as this is the medium in which they operate, while that used by the latter allow the paratroopers to communicate while they are in the air before landing. In comple-

COMMUNICATIONS SYSTEMS

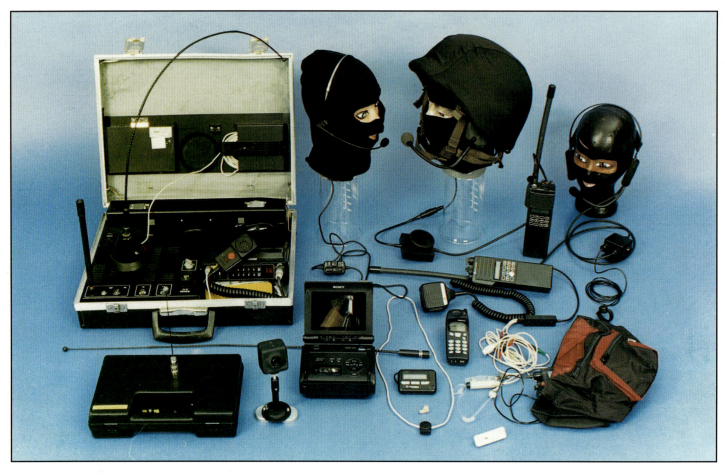

mentary actions, ranging from operations associated with the explosive activation/deactivation teams to operations necessary to provide personal protection/security, normally walkie-talkie-type receiver-transmitters are deployed that combine the characteristics of lightness, multiple band frequency, confidentiality and low cost.

The upper range includes vehicle radios and other systems, which generally operate at bands such as VHF (Very High Frequency) or UHF (Ultra High Frequency). They facilitate communication with the upper echelons in command or with police and government authorities that may be involved in the operation. This equipment allows communication over distances of several hundred kilometers. The use of digital mobile phones is also spreading, as they are light and allow conversation over open channels.

Options on the market
There are many companies manufacturing communication equipment which include in their product lines systems spe-

Varied range
A police assault group needs a variety of communications and monitoring devices. Proof of this is the display shown here of the material used by the URNA, special police of the Czech Republic, in carrying out their missions.

cifically designed for use in this type of high-level police activity, as well as elements that could be used by special police.

The United States Option
Of all the firms in the United States, one firm stands out, Motorola Incorporated, with its manufacturing plants in Schaumburg and Bloomingdale, Illinois. Their most renowned equipment is the Saber portable radio, of which they manufacture several models that are remarkable for the fact that they include up to 120 channels (model III), are manufactured of water-resistant materials and can be equipped with the Securenet system, allowing privacy in voice messages. Their MTS 2000 model can be updated

Equipment used by the Germans
The special operations groups of the German Polizei use systems such as this Mastercom, including an activator situated on a finger of the left hand to prevent officers from distraction from their principal task in order to connect by radio.

COMMUNICATIONS SYSTEMS

with a special software linked to its FLASHport system and can be chosen in VHF, UHF, 800 or 900 megahertz frequency bands. they also sell ACT-101 advanced communication terminals; MX-340 y 350 systems, which operate at VHF and include cryptography, and MX-100 protected systems for work in the marine environment.

Other US models used by these units include the LASH II earphone/microphone set by Television Equipment Associates, consisting of an integrated headphone set placed inside the ear and a transmitter attached to the neck to receive the vibrations of the speaker. The same firm also produces other systems, including the TASC system, with earphones and microphone, attached to the head with an elastic strap, the SKWRC (Swimmer's Kit Waterproof Radio Container), specially designed for divers who must descend to depths of up to 15 meters, or the DAED (Davies Active Ear Defender), earphones that filter loud noises caused by explosions or gunfire but allow noise at normal conversation levels to be heard.

Optimized models

Another important firm with its headquarters in Great Britain is Davies Industrial Communications Limited, a firm producing TACMIC CT connectors, facilitating links between radios, microphones and earphones and providing user-friendly activation; the CT400 system, consisting of different types of ear and microphones depending on the customer's needs, and including an adapter for use with oxygen masks, and the OSK bag, designed to carry a radio and keep it dry in underwater operations.

The IC-R2, IC-R10 and IC-F30 radios, manufactured by the Japanese firm Icom, are compact and advanced, as well as sensitive and light models, to which various accessories can be adapted. Also reliable are radios by the French firm Maxon, which manufactures models such as Niros TRX 1012 CENELEC, that can be programmed to connect with up to one hundred channels.

The Ericsson firm, with headquarters in Sweden, manufactures systems such as KPC, M-RK and NPC-200, the latter being a compact radio with aluminum body and sixteen channels designed to comply with 810 D&E standard military specifications, that can transmit at 1.4 to 5 watts as the case may be. Other specific offers on the market include micro-earphones such as the R-5 model, placed inside the outer ear so that they are hidden from sight; microphones such as the SK-3, that can be attached to a finger to facilitate discrete activation; systems such as the SK-7, that are attached to the collar of a garment to hide it, or radios such as the MC 9600 by the French firm, Matra Nortel Communications. Cofrexport, from the same country, is specialized in mobile systems installed in briefcases to facilitate their deployment, and that can transmit through both through land stations and satellites such as INMARSAT.

Support equipment
The vans used to transport US SWAT team members, such as this one belonging to an Arizona team, are equipped with computerized terminals to establish contact with the base, mobile telephones and battery recharging devices for the members' personal equipment.

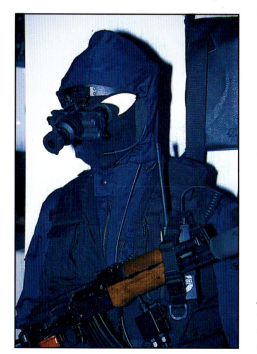

Many manufacturers
The production of special equipment is focussed in a select group of Western countries, although some equipment like this is produced in Eastern European countries.

PHOENIX PD SPECIAL RESPONSE TEAM

The particular idiosyncrasy of the United States with regard to national security has led to the creation of police departments that are fully equipped with all possible means necessary for carrying out their duty. The ratio of agents per thousand inhabitants and the cost per capita for this service are remarkable.

Along these lines, the Police Department (PD) of the city of Phoenix, Arizona –ranked sixth in size in the country– has a complex and self-sufficient organizational structure that allows it to handle all sorts of incidents. It has a special group trained for assault and arrest operations: the Special Response Team

Shared expertise
All of the members of the Unit are qualified to act as snipers, but only a few stand out from the rest for their superior skill in handling this type of firearms in situations requiring good psychological control and high physical resistance.

(SRT), a Unit which is ranked third in the United States insofar as size and capacity for action.

Police model
Phoenix is one of the larger cities in

Firing power
The Steyr AUG P assault rifle is a compact, effective and precise weapon used by the Phoenix police force to handle dangerous situations both by day or night, during which a Sure-Fire flashlight mounted on the barrel is very helpful.

the US, with a population of over one million spread throughout a large surface area of approximately five hundred and fifty square miles filled with single family houses. The Police Department, which was founded in 1871, has three thousand officers or so, plus five hundred people as support staff in charge of administrative or maintenance tasks. It has been entrusted with insuring the safety of the inhabitants through their half dozen police stations located throughout the populated area.

Special group
A small group of officers comprise the Special Assignments Unit (SAU), which, since it was established in 1961,

PHOENIX PD SPECIAL RESPONSE TEAM

FLASH-BANG STUN GRENADES

The need to enter buildings which are suspected to contain armed people who could fire against other civilians in the area, against hostages, or against the police officers executing the assault themselves, calls for the use of devices to reduce the criminals' response level or distract them from the principal action taken against them.

One of these devices is the Def-Tec, model 25 stun grenade, used by the Phoenix SRT members, who value their light weight, ease of use after removing the safety pin and being thrown towards the area where they are to detonate, and their noteworthy effectiveness. The latter characteristic is due to the one or more very loud detonations (170 decibels) they produce, at specific times after activation, depending on the model (there are models with two or three-second delays or more). This affects the ears of people nearby considerably, and neutralizes their hearing capacity for a short time. At the same time, it also produces several very intense flashes which reach a brightness of 2.5 million candelas and temporarily blind the adversary. The combined effect of the noise and the blinding light is enough to produce a paralysis of several seconds, a period which is used by the officers to subdue the criminals and prevent them from firing or activating a previously-prepared explosive device.

provides specially chosen, trained and equipped forces to handle police situations that are beyond the scope of the regular force.

The SAU consists of: a K-9 team, with police using dogs specially trained for locating drugs or explosives, and German Shepherds trained for preceding assault groups and attacking (a task in which several dogs have been killed); a Bomb Squadron, with specialists who operate sophisticated remote control robots and use trailers specially designed for the safe transport of suspicious packages; and an assault team. The latter is known as the Special Response Team (SRT), led by a Lieutenant as the Commander in Chief and consists of thirty or so professionals –two of them women– who are divided into four assault teams who are on duty in eight-hour shifts (morning, afternoon and night) five days a week.

They can be called to duty immediately through a complex system of calls and beepers. They respond within an hour from having been alerted for a new mission, which implies that all members must be available at all times and live near the precinct headquarters to which they are assigned. Nonetheless, there are always two teams on call who are available for response within half an hour.

Each assault group consists of a Sergeant and seven officers who usually operate together and in a coordinated manner, which is very important in carrying out missions and being able to predict other team members' reactions. Their general training is similar because they have all followed the same initial training process, but they also have ongoing training to maintain their specialization.

The Command acts as "Point" or leader, one officer is in charge of protecting the advance of the rest with the aid of a thick armored shield in a task known as "Point Cover", two are qualified to act as snipers, firing against targets up to half a kilometer away –it should be kept in mind that the flatlands of Arizona often make approaching the target area difficult–, one has trained and is skilled in negotiating with abductors or people holding hostages in order to convince them to desist without the use of force, two are in charge of using grenade launchers to fire bombs that emit irritating or neutralizing gases to facilitate the intervention of the other officers in solving incidents, and the rest of the members knows how to use special components such as communications equipment or night sights perfectly.

Demonstrated professionalism

Their training begins when they are admitted to the Phoenix Police Training Academy, a training center for future police officers. In compliance with the regulations of the Arizona Law Enforcement Academy (ALEA), which stipulates the aspects that must be covered in training programs for members of public security forces, students follow a 15 week program of 600 lesson hours covering both physical training as well as

PHOENIX PD SPECIAL RESPONSE TEAM

subjects such as arrests, criminal law, patrol procedure, the Constitution, Justice Administration, traffic, first aid, organized crime, homicide, radio procedures and defensive driving, to name just a few.

Those who pass this stage are admitted to the Phoenix PD and go on to carry out their duties in one of the various divisions of the Police Department. Every so often, there is an opening for the SRT, depending on available space. Many professional officers apply, attracted by the special tasks carried out by this team.

As prerequisites, candidates must: have served at least three years on the police force; pass physical tests attempting to select the most athletic and tough-

Coordinated maneuvers
The assault team members must move in a quick and coordinated manner in order to avoid being hit by criminal fire, and to carry out their missions with greater assurance of success.

Covered advance
While a partner holds a heavy armored shield with NATO-2 capacity to withstand any bullet fired from an assault rifle, two other SRT officers aim at the target, knowing that they are partially covered from enemy fire.

est people; complete a test on general knowledge; and undergo a series of psychotechnological tests, given to ascertain those individuals capable of rapid, professional and safe response. Those selected follow an initial training program for the Unit, given to them by the other, non-novice members of the Unit, who teach them the daily tasks they carry out and the means available, and provide a theoretical-practical base principally relating handling and use of firearms.

Once they have finished this stage, they are sent to one of the schools specializing in teaching aspects on tactics and special weapons within the police field. In the United States there are many such academies, whether private or public, pro-

viding progressive training lasting from two weeks to several months, depending on the level of training desired.

They then become members of the operative teams of the Unit, where they

PHOENIX PD SPECIAL RESPONSE TEAM

complete their training through sessions with their colleagues, members who have an average of ten years' professional experience with the SRT. Daily training includes exercises in the precinct's gymnasium or running to maintain their physical fitness, practicing at the firing range with their assigned personal weapons as well as with other group weapons, and attending meetings where new developments in tactics or equipment are discussed.

Every month they must pass a firing examination that is very tough, as they could be sued by citizens should they commit an act of negligence during a mission which is due to their not meeting required standards. They also travel to

Covering his partner
A police officer points his MP5 submachine gun at a door while his partner aims at a hinge with his 12 caliber shotgun, with which he will fire several rounds in order to knock the door down with ease, quickly proceeding to enter the building.

Protected travel
This armored vehicle, ceded by the US Air Force, is very useful for approaching areas of conflict and deploying the six officers who can travel in the rear compartment. It is equipped with spotlights that can be moved from inside to illuminate specific areas.

specific locations or training centers to carry out exercises in assault, freeing of hostages, neutralization of criminals or use of grenades, with snipers carrying out additional training with their precision weapons.

Their general training is complemen-

PHOENIX PD SPECIAL RESPONSE TEAM

Physical preparation
The members of the Phoenix Special Response Team keep themselves in the best physical condition through various activities, including the regular use of their complete gymnasium.

ted by practice sessions on the Department's helicopters, travel to other cities to study real operations of significance carried out there, collaboration with similar groups from other Departments or with the local agents of the Federal Bureau of Investigation (FBI), and continual missions in support of the detectives that need their help for arrest operations involving a high degree of risk. Every year they attend fifty or so calls to intervene in their specialty, and participate in one hundred and twenty or so search entries to arrest criminals, 90 % of these related to narcotics. Since the creation of the SRT, three of its officers have been reached by the adversary's fire, and the officers have killed six people.

Rapid movements
McDonnell Douglas 520 Notar helicopters are a useful instrument for transporting team members to an operation point. They are readily available for SRT use, which makes transport even quicker.

Special weapons
In order to carry out their duties, whether alone or in groups, and handle criminals, the officers are always equipped with the weapons necessary for the assigned mission. The range of systems and equipment placed at their disposal is very wide, and includes both the weapons

PHOENIX PD SPECIAL RESPONSE TEAM

Protected advance
A thick, armored NATO-2 shield, capable of withstanding .308 Winchester caliber rounds, is the tool used by the Phoenix police to advance in scenarios in which it is highly likely they will be fired against.

Shock JHP, with 147 grain tips that deform a great deal and have a great stopping power, it being the same cartridge used in MP5 submachine guns by the German firm Heckler und Koch. The latter is also part of their personal equipment, their arsenal including both the A4 variant, equipped with a fixed buttstock made of plastic, and the A5 variant, with a retractile metallic stock. More effective than the SD model, a silencer manufactured by the firm AWC Systems Technology can be attached to the muzzle of the MP5s to considerably reduce the report produced when firing. This element can be used when the tactical situation calls for it and is best when used with subsonic ammunition to increase its effectiveness.

Much more powerful, and more useful for handling situations in which the opponents are armed with high-caliber weapons or are wearing bulletproof vests, the Steyr AUG Police assault rifle fires in semiautomatic mode (single shot), using 5.56x45 mm caliber rounds, thirty or forty-two of which fit into its plastic, semitransparent cartridges. A mount has been installed on their front end on which to attach Sure-Fire flashlights to illuminate dark areas and verify whether the subject who is to be fired at is armed or not.

that comprise their personal equipment as well as those available for the group in general.

Contrasted efficiency
The Department has selected the famous P226 semiautomatic, by the Swiss firm Sig Sauer, as their official pistol. This model fires 9x19 millimeter Parabellum ammunition, with the magazine holding fifteen plus one in the chamber. In addition, SRT members can choose other models of the same caliber, including the Italian Beretta 92s or the Austrian Glock, models 17, 19 and 26, the latter being ultra-compact and therefore easily concealed as a secondary short weapon.

The ammunition used in this type of semiautomatics is called Federal Hydra

Constant training
The four teams that comprise the Phoenix SRT keep up an intensive training program in areas such as shooting, tactical deployment and coordinated movements, exercises that they carry out regularly to maintain their high level.

PHOENIX PD SPECIAL RESPONSE TEAM

Also on hand are Colt M16 Carbines with retractile buttstock and a shorter handguard, a weapon that, like the previously mentioned ones, also fires .223 caliber rounds of Federal Premium BTHP type, with 55 grain tips that are effective and have sufficient penetration capacity such that they do not perforate thin walls separating rooms in a house. Breaking a hinge, destroying a lock or detaining a car that attempts to escape a control are some of the tasks in which Remington slide-action shotguns come in handy. They can be equipped with a buttstock with a pistol grip that allows them to be held more easily. This weapon takes 12/70 or 12/76 caliber Magnum that correspond to the Federal standard in a configuration loaded with 9 double zero pellets or 2 3/4 inch Slug-type bullets.

Snipers are assigned Remington 700 rifles of 7.62x51 mm caliber, weapons equipped with a heavy barrel, Kevlar and graphite buttstocks, Harris bipod and Leupold optical sight with 3.5-10x50 power to achieve maximum precision within a range of up to six hundred meters, using Federal Mach cartridges equipped with Sierra BTHP, 168 grain tips characterized by their notable precision and great effectiveness.

Quick transport

To guarantee reaching any point of the wide metropolitan area of Phoenix with speed, considering that its highways are often jammed with traffic and distances can be up to twenty or thirty miles, helicopters of the Aviation Unit are often used, whose operative and maintenance headquarters are located at an airport for small private aircraft in the northern part of the city. The Aviation Unit is assigned half a dozen McDonnell Douglas 520N Notar helicopters, two of which are always kept on alert or flown in surveillance and observation flights. This air-

Trained police dogs
The K-9 Section includes several dogs and their trainers. These dogs are specially trained for locating explosives, drugs or people. Some are also trained in attack and arrest techniques applied to people suspected of having committed a crime.

Snipers
We can see one of the professionals in charge of high precision firing at a range of more than 500 meters aiming his Remington 700 bolt-action rifle at a target. These professionals generally choose a high point from which to control the situation.

PHOENIX PD SPECIAL RESPONSE TEAM

craft can transport four officers each at a maximum speed of approximately two hundred kilometers per hour, which guarantees their arrival at the scene of an incident in few minutes.

Its small size, its piped tail rotor system and low noise level of its engine also contribute to its tactical use, while officers can be transported on the skids holding on to specially designed handles for greater safety. It can also help in deployment with rappel rope. For night missions, FLIR (Forward Looking Infra Red) system is very useful. Located under the fuselage, it is connected to a video screen showing the heat imprint of the image captured by the system.

Also contributing to their rapid deployment is the fact that some of the special police on duty often patrol conflictive areas with a partner, dressed as civilians so as not to be identified. Their transport means is an unmarked van with cabinets in the rear for carrying equipment, a space reserved for the complex communications equipment, benches that can be turned into beds for resting on those missions that last longer than usual, and even a small refrigerator and an electric coffee machine that make life more comfortable.

For group travel, they use large vans with two long benches for transporting up to two police teams, with the specific equipment that might be required for the mission being transported in another, specially adapted van that is unmarked so as not to be easily identified. Inside, perfectly organized in specific compartments, it can carry: lighting materials with generators, cables and portable spotlights; assault equipment such as poles with sights, metal shears, battering rams and explosives; electrical material for operations such as, for example, manipulating the ignition system of a car to make it stop running when the officers decide, so that the abductors cannot flee the scene of the crime; communications systems with radio, telephone and

TACTICAL HOLSTER

Several American firms, among which Galco stands out for the top quality products they manufacture at their plant in Phoenix, offer their customers tactical holsters for carrying short weapons. Among the wide range and abundance of options is the leg model used by the Phoenix SRT members, which is designed to provide carrying ease and rapid access for this secondary weapon.
The holster is attached at the top to the right side of the police officer's belt, and at the bottom to the right thigh, such that it is firmly in place and does not move. This is an ideal position for taking out the pistol without making strange movements, because it only requires the user to stretch out his/her arm, undo the upper strap that keeps the pistol from falling, and pull it upwards to extract it. Made in a combination of highly durable synthetic materials, this model is equipped with an adjustment knob, a screw, that can be coupled to various models of short weapons so that they are securely held in place and cannot fall out during the operations that these professionals carry out.

PHOENIX PD "SPECIAL RESPONSE TEAM"

speaker components; emergency aid equipment with safety suits against fire, harnesses, ropes and stretchers for transporting injured people, and bottles of compressed air for breathing in contaminated areas; riot materials such as 37 mm Ferret tear gas launchers which shoot smoke bombs for concealment or tear gas bombs; and various other equipment such as Litton M911A night sights and headphones and microphones for listening in on conversations from a safe distance.

Of a similar size are the trucks used by the K-9 team or the bomb squadron, a group which is assigned a remote-control caterpillar robot known as "Sweet Pea"

Command Center
The "Mobile Activity Command" is a large van that has been adapted and equipped with communications and situation overview systems that help the management of a crisis situation.

Safe transport
The "Bomb disposal" is a spherical titanium container that has been designed to move independently through all sorts of places. Explosive devices can be placed inside through this small, 50 centimeter door, to neutralize the effects of their detonation.

(Popeye's son), a trailer with an armored compartment for transporting explosive devices to places where they can be neutralized or detonated, and the Nabco TCBDU (Total Containment Bomb Disposal Unit) self-propelled container, made of titanium to withstand the detonation of up to 4.5 kilograms of explosives, placed inside it through a lateral,

PHOENIX PD "SPECIAL RESPONSE TEAM"

Practical class
The facilities where the "Aviation Unit" is stationed are located in an airport in the northern part of the city, and comprise a series of buildings and open ground used for carrying out all sort of group training exercises.

electrically operated hatch, without deformation. Its great mobility makes it very useful, as it can move through elevators, hallways and rooms independently.

In special situations in which armed conflict may occur, or to reach the point from which a sniper is firing on people, a four-wheel drive armored vehicle is used, received as surplus from the Air Force and equipped with a chassis capable of withstanding the impact of rounds fired from any assault rifle. It can hold two drivers and a group of six officers. As additional support for SAU operations, a large van can be used that has been adapted as a mobile command center, called Mobile Activity Command.

Personal gear
In their training and operations, these officers wear a navy blue outfit consisting of a pair of pants and a loose shirt made of a combination of cotton and synthetic fibers for added durability, the loose shirt often being substituted by a short-sleeve shirt in many activities due to the extreme heat that is the norm nearly year-round in Arizona. Over this, they wear the Phoenix Vest model of the Hoffman Enterprises tactical jacket, which includes various pockets for all sorts of accessories and large identifying police emblems. It is made of Kevlar, lending it a level III deterrence capacity under normal conditions, and level IV if combined with large ceramic plates inserted in specially designed pockets.

Their personal gear also includes a Kevlar helmet corresponding to the military model PASGT (Personal Armor System Ground Troops) but painted black. At the waist they wear a belt with a Galco leg holster for their pistol. They cover their faces with a face mask to conceal their identity, and Stemaco safety glasses over their eyes for protection against wind and small impacts, while their feet are protected by police intervention boots with a flat, anti-skid sole.

Other basic work gear includes gloves to protect their hands and for a better grip on their weapons, rappel harnesses for greater security in their movements, Eagle personal communications equipment, interconnected with Motorola MTS2000 and Ericcson radios, Sure-Fire illumination lights, either hand-held or attached to the weapon, MSA gas masks with the filter at the side to facilitate firing with long weapons, and personal beepers that allow officers to receive messages at all times.

Data processing
Some of the vehicles assigned to the Unit are equipped with terminals and screens that allow information to be gathered on the sites under surveillance. They can even be used to download the floor plans of the site from the municipal registry.

PHOENIX PD "SPECIAL RESPONSE TEAM"

Remote control
This caterpillar-track robot is remote-controlled and equipped with spotlights, video cameras, shotgun and a pincer. It is used to locate, observe, move or neutralize packages or vehicles suspected of containing explosive devices.

Auxiliary tool
37 millimeter single-fire grenade launchers can fire various types of devices at a considerable distance. The grenades it launches are usually loaded with tear or smoke gas (or at times with rubber pellets) that can help resolve specific incidents.

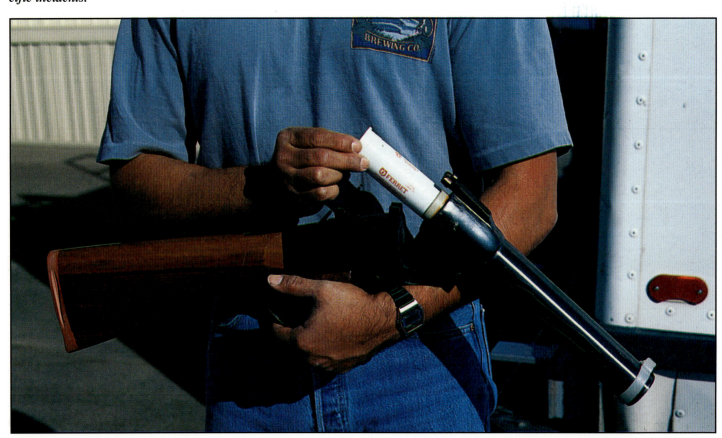

SNIPERS

After a seven-hour wait, the officers' muscles and joints are stiff. A police group sniper keeps the reference point he has taken as his target in sight, which is a criminal holding a group of people hostage in a bank. Events develop and, to prevent the individual from acting against a hostage, he receives the order to fire. The criminal's profile allows the sniper to choose the lower ear, which is very vulnerable due to its proximity to the spinal chord. He holds his breath for several seconds, then softly presses the trigger, activating the hammer which causes the detonation of the cartridge..

Personal gear
Police snipers have a wide range of gear available, that they take with them during training exercises and operational deployment, which supports them in their task.

At approximately eight hundred meters per second, the bullet begins its trajectory, which ends in brief tenths of a second, after going through the glass of a window and having impact on the subject, who instantly falls to the floor, at which time the assault group makes a

Silent
Spanish GEO force members have been assigned Sako TRG21 precision rifles, equipped with an integrated barrel/silencer assembly that notably reduces the report otherwise produced by the 7.62x51 mm cartridges that they fire.

SNIPERS

Maximum precision
This GEO sniper is aiming at a target with a 5.56 caliber semiautomatic rifle. In order to stabilize the weapon, the metallic bipod is very useful. It is integrated in the handguard and retracts for easy transport.

rapid entrance and controls the situation. The incident is over and none of the hostages was injured. The operation, after many hours of negotiation, is considered a success.

Constant preparation

To make this possible, many months –or even years– of training and specialization were necessary in an activity that requires a great deal of sang froid, skill at keeping calm for long periods of time, mastering the weapon assigned and knowing the limits of precision shooting with regards to the external factors that can affect the trajectory of a bullet in flight.

Initial selection

To select elite snipers for a special police unit, the candidates' characteristics must be considered, including, for some police units, personal aspects such as having a high intelligence quotient, have a great capacity for observation or being a non-smoker. In principle, it could also be positive to have practiced target shooting as a civilian, especially when the candidate has demonstrated the capacity to handle this type of arms and get the maximum out of them.

Another aspect which is considered is the character demonstrated during the initial preparation stage as an officer in a special assault group, a preparation which includes firing with all sorts of weapons and allows those to be selected who demonstrate a greater predisposition, according to the results obtained, to act as snipers.

Once the first group of candidates has been selected, a training stage takes place which covers both theoretical and practical subjects. Theoretical subjects include operational procedures, the factors that condition shooting, projectile ballistics studies, information on diverse types of ammunition, evaluation of slide-operated weapons vs. semiautomatic ones, the sniper's gear, calculation of distance to the target and use of measuring means, regulation of daytime optical sights and use of nocturnal optronics, simultaneous firing procedures, firing techniques in adverse lighting conditions, and a long list of subjects that are usually given at the base or in specialized institutions, among which are the US Thunder Ranch, Gunsite or STTU (Specialized Tactical Training Unit), directed by Mark V. Lonsdale.

Practical subjects are usually studied in parallel with the theoretical classes and include a process of familiarization with the weapons assigned to the Unit, which begins with firing ranges at small distances of between 50 and 100 meters. After a time, the setting is changed and tactical deployment exercises are inclu-

Accuracy
The US firm Robar produces the SR60 and SR90 rifle series, that are used by various Police Departments in the United States and in other countries, weapons that stand out for their finish and their notable accuracy.

ERGONOMIC BUTTSTOCK

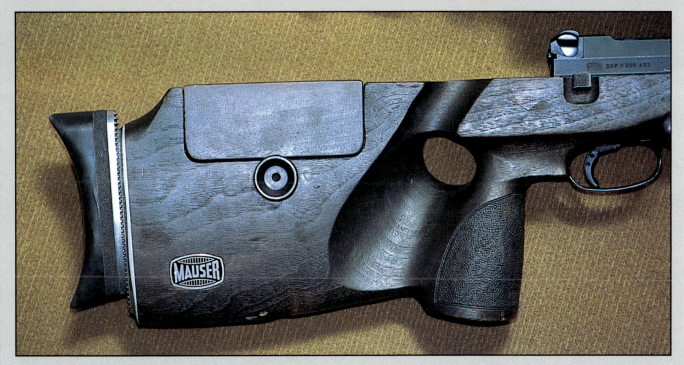

The great majority of police precision rifles have a buttstock specially designed to allow a total symbiosis between the weapon and the user, a symbiosis depending on the rifle perfectly adapting to the grip of the holder to achieve the highest precision. Absolutely ergonomic buttstocks are manufactured to meet this need, which come in both wood or plastic derivatives. There are numerous models on the market by reputed US manufacturers such as Robar, McMillan or HS Precision.
Basically, the buttstock is equipped with special features that constitute the weapon's most significant qualities.

In its upper front part, it has a large groove that leaves the barrel free and allows for a perfect float so that the barrel can oscillate freely after each shot. Its lower front end is rounded to allow for better grip and includes fittings for attaching a bipod or tripod that provide better stability, while the rear is equipped with mobile adjustment elements including a piece adjustable to the user's face and a corner unit adjustable for depth and height, all of which allows for a better adaptation to the police officer's body.

ded, working on the difficulty of aiming in the most varied conditions, in which there is a positive or negative gradient between the sniper and the target, elements which make aiming and viewing the target difficult. Sometimes even simulated civilians are placed in the target area, and the distance is progressively increased until the maximum suggested distance is reached, depending on the caliber of the weapon, which at 5.56x45 millimeters is a distance of 300 m, and up to 700 m in the case of the 7.62x51 mm, 1,200 m with .338 Lapua Magnum or .300 Winchester Magnum and nearly two kilometers with rifles of 12.70x99 (.50 Browning) caliber.

Personal gear

Many activities can be entrusted to police snipers, who usually work in groups of two, depending on the personnel available at each department. Their tasks can include observing the target area and informing superiors of what is occurring, gather information to plan an assault, cover the assault team and provide security, protect medical personnel when these are needed, hit targets selected by commanders or fire distracting shots, among other things.

In order to accomplish these varied tasks, that are carried out during operations against terrorist elements or abductors and on protective missions, specific gear is assigned them, which normally includes a comfortable uniform, which can be in one piece, various means of observation including binoculars or telescopes, especially those that are compact in size and include a quality lens with great magnifying power, elements to improve their position such as firing blankets or stabilization sacks to rest the weapon on, sophisticated communications equipment –especially that which does not require the use of hands– allowing them to maintain several channels open with their superiors and with those coordinating the snipers, and cleaning implements to facilitate preparation of

SNIPERS

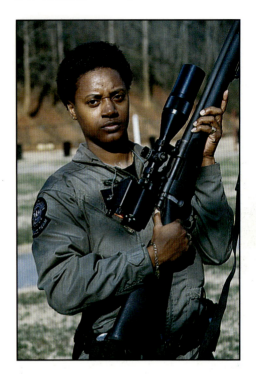

the weapon after its use and to eliminate any residues of gunpowder or dirt.

Also needed are cases resistant to impacts for transporting the weapon, small backpacks or waist packs in which to carry accessories such as fluids for hydration or high energy foods in case the wait is prolonged, camouflage body suits or other camouflage elements that allow them to go undetected when operations take place in rural settings, bipods and tripods with which to stabilize rifles that are aimed at a target, warm clothing and protection should the weather call for them, optical or laser telemeters to measure the distance from the target with precision, firing gloves, various types of ammunition in order to adapt shots to the concrete characteristics of each target, and personal protection weapons to confer additional security during deployment.

Also very important is the notebook or booklet where each sniper has kept notes from practice on exercises and the results obtained with each variation of position and situation. Reading these notes will allow them to be more precise when carrying out real operations, and they can add details of the planning of the specific activity, operational and contingency plans, and other procedural details that may have been established in previous meetings or briefings.

In any conditions
The SWAT team in Atlanta uses 2.5 to 10-power ITT optical sights that include an optronic residual light intensifier module that can be mounted on the sight to enable both daytime and nighttime shooting.

Selecting the weapon

Those responsible for special assault units integrated into Security Forces or Police Departments must consider various factors when selecting the equipment which they will assign their snipers. The calibers to be used must be considered, what degree of precision is to be required of the weapon, what the most ideal method of operation is, what accessories are to be required for its use and, most importantly, what are the economic means available for acquisition and the number of weapons needed.

Many models

Depending on the previous criteria, and others that may be established for particular cases, selections can be made of models manufactured by well-known European or US manufacturers that are specialized in manufacturing arms complying with strict police specifications and notably different from rifles used by sports shooters or hunters.

Of the weapons available, the widest offer is in manually-operated rifles with a lock, moved by the sniper, who activates a lateral lever to move a cartridge from the magazine to the chamber. This slow process has the advantage of easy handling and the total security that the cartridge, visible to the user, is located in firing position. Among US manufacturers, one of the best firms is Robar, directed by Robbie Barrkman at his production center in Phoenix, Arizona, where they produce models such as SR-60 and SR-90, that stand out for their heavy or floating barrels, ergonomic buttstocks and capacity to carry out groupings at less than _ MOA (Minute of Angle); something like grouping several impacts in a square of a little more than a centimeter per side at 100 meters from the position of the sniper.

Also famous are the products manufactured by McMillan based on Remington 700 type action, among the best of which are weapons such as the M-86SR and M-89SR the barrel of which is equipped with built-in silencer. Other Ameri-

Barricades
Any urban element, such as this wall and pipe, can be used by these professionals to take up comfortable and stable positions from which to shoot with maximum accuracy.

SNIPERS

Rooftops
The rooftops of buildings constitute a vantage point from which snipers can aim their weapons comfortably, covering a wide range on security missions that they may be entrusted.

can models are the Remington M700 Police of .308 caliber, used by various agencies, and H-S Precision products, that have a good reputation for their buttstock combining Kevlar with graphite so that it is lighter and stronger.

In Europe, bolt-operated rifles are very common, such as the Austrian Steyr-Mannlicher SSG, which come in various finishes; Finnish Sako rifles of TRG type, offered in basic models 21 and 41, with short and long-action, respectively; the French Hecate, including weapons designed to fire the powerful .50 Browning acquired by the GIGN Squad of the French Police Corps; or German ones such as the Mauser 66, 86 or 93, part of various Spanish, Portuguese and Italian units' arsenal. Other interesting models are the Swiss SSG 2000 and 3000, designed to offer the best ergonomics and precision, or the British AW by the firm Accuracy International, that are beginning to appear in police arsenals after military units became interested in them. The same firm has also manufactured the

Optional accessories
The Finnish firm Sako produces excellent bolt-action rifles, such as the .308 Winchester caliber TRG21 shown in the photo, which can be fitted with a silencer that is screwed onto the end of the barrel.

SNIPERS

Careful design
Heckler und Koch semiautomatic rifles, model 33, include the variant SG/1, optimized to function as a short-range precision weapon. Noteworthy are the rear slide, the sight mount, the front bipod and various shooting accessories.

new, 12.70 caliber AW50F, that can come with a retractable buttstock, while another British firm, Parker Hale, offers the M98.

Semiautomatic rifles are noisier than manually-operated ones because they use some of the gases accompanying the projectile to move the mechanisms that expel the shell and introduce a new cartridge in the chamber. One of the most outstanding among these is the German Heckler und Koch (H&K) PSG-1, a totally reliable weapon that stands out for being as accurate as a bolt-operated rifle due to its excellent polygonal barrel and its capacity to fire sequential shots with great speed. It costs somewhat over $ 6.000 for the piece without sights, and so is not affordable to all budgets.

Other H&K products are more economic, including the 33 SG/1 and the MSG90 and G3 SG/1, the former using 5.56 caliber cartridges whereas the latter uses 7.62 caliber cartridges. The Swiss SSG550 are also very precise, and are remarkable for their 65 cm barrel length.

The US industry produces curious transformations of the mechanism used to equip the 7.62 caliber M14 military rifle, a robust mechanism that has been tried over many years. Weapons manufactured with said mechanism are built with Mach-type barrels such as those made by Douglas, and ergonomic buttstocks optimized to improve aim and accuracy, capable of achieving groups of 1 MOA. Among models available are the M29, manufactured by AWC Systems Technology, standing out for its adjustable buttstock and its pistol-type grip, and those manufactured by Springfield, which continues to produce the M21, that was originally designed for military use. In the US, diverse transformations of the AR-15/M16 are also carried out to achieve significant groups at short range, because its small caliber – .223 Remington- is only efficient at a radius of 60 to 100 meters, within which its ammunition, such as the new TAP (Tactical Application Police), can reach its maximum potential in precision and expansion of the projectile upon impact.

Telescopic sights for all budgets

For the above-mentioned weapons to reach the potential of precision guaranteed by the manufacturers, they must be fitted with the appropriate sight with the necessary lens quality and power. A telescopic sight with a magnifying power of 30, for example, is not normally placed on a 5.56 mm weapon, nor is a sight with a power of 4 placed on a 12.70 rifle. The offer available is very wide, but the good models are very expensive, on ave-

Constantly in communication
Police group snipers take up the most favorable positions for shooting, stabilize their weapons with sacks or bipods and wait for orders to act, using their communications equipment to keep constantly informed of what events.

SNIPERS

Concealed
When police snipers must take action in rural settings, they often wear camouflage uniforms and other camouflage elements such as the American ghillie suit that this police officer is wearing to prevent his detection.

rage surpassing US$ 800 for those manufactured in the US, and US$ 2,000 for those made in Europe, with those devices capable of amplifying residual light to allow night shooting costing five times as much.

Police groups have adopted sight brands such as the German Zeiss-Diavari or Hensoldt, which assiduously accompany H&K rifles. Among the former firm's options are an 8x56 mm model, while the latter offers one of 6x42 mm. Other highly reputable manufacturers are Schmidt & Bender, offering the 3-12x50 Police/Marksman II, a widespread model that can be acquired with Bryant or mildot type reticles; Swarovski, with its 2.5-10x42 and 3-12x50; and the Austrian firm Karl Khales with models such as ZF95los Helia 6x42, 8x50 and 8x56.

On this side of the Atlantic, one manufacturer stands out above the rest: Leupold, a company that manufactures quality sights at a very satisfactory price.

Constant training
This sniper from the Forth Worth SWAT team in Texas is aiming his 7.62x51 mm caliber Remington rifle at a target during one of the team's numerous shooting exercises that allow them to maintain very high personal and professional skill levels.

Its most renowned models include the Mark 4 10x40 Ultra, available with various different reticles, the Vari X III 3.5-10X50 Police or the Tactical 3.5-10x40, to which can be added the latest models, the 6.5-20x50 and 6.6-25x50 for very long range firing.

For night shooting, optronic sight elements are used, or modules that can be attached to optical sights that are affixed to the weapon. Among the former are the well-known US AN/PVS4 sight, using a 2nd generation light intensifier tube and was created in response to a military request; the various models manufactured by the Litton firm, including the M845 line and the M937/M938; the British firm, Pilkington Optronics, with compact models; and Italian products manufactured by Aeri-

SNIPERS

talia and Officine Galileo.

The latter have the advantage that they are attached to a flat piece above the optical sight, so that adjustment of the reticular cross hair that designates the foreseen point of impact is not necessary. Some of the best among these are the versatile Norwegian Simrad, available in various configurations which adapt to different day sight models. One of its most remarkable features is that it is available with either 2nd or 3rd generation tubes. Those manufactured by the US company ITT are more compact, including sight models such as the F7201A, that is equipped with a 2.5-10x56 mm optical element and a capturing module of 408 grams with an infrared illuminator that screws onto the rear quickly and easily, so that an officer could carry the piece in a small protective cover and screw it on should the tactical situation or lack of light so require.

SIMRAD NOCTURNAL MODULE

The firm Simrad Optronics A/S, based in Oslo, Sweden, manufactures various light-intensifying modules whose basic feature is that they can be attached to diverse sight elements to allow the user to see both by day and by night. With models such as KN200, KN202 or KN250, this family of products consists of a large cylinder –the latest model, last in the list, measures 188 mm in length by 136 in height and 105 in width– and is equipped with a wide-view catadioptric front lens piece protected by an oscillating cover, an attachment fitting on the lower front for attachment in front of the weapons optical sight, a capturing tube in the middle holding the alkaline batteries that provide nearly 100 hours of continuous use, and the control and adjustment knobs.
On its underside it has two fixtures allowing attachment to the corresponding fixtures on the upper part of the optical visor, so that the sniper uses the latter during the day and the light-capturing module in adverse light conditions. It need only be attached to the upper part of the sight, the protective cover removed and the module activated to be able to use a light amplifier that, depending on whether it is 2nd or 3rd generation, will allow taking sight of a target without making any additional adjustments, as the reticle's cross hair remain fixed.

THE SPECIAL OPERATIONS SECTION OF ATLANTA

Assault
The elevated crime rate that the main cities of the United States suffer has caused Police Departments to establish special units, of which Atlanta's is remarkable for its significance and preparation.

In mid-1999, a tragic event occurred in Atlanta, the capital of the state of Georgia. The 44 year old stockbroker Mark Burton, feeling frustrated for having suffered high economic losses, became yet another American who lost his mind and fired against civilians. First it was against his wife and two children, who died as a result. Then he went to the agency where he worked and began firing left and right; he killed nine people and injured another 13.

The alarm caused by the shots coming from the building activated the enormous police force directed by Police Chief Beverly J. Harvard, and as quickly as possible, officers who had been patrolling in the area reached the scene first, rapidly followed by members of the Special Weapons and Tactics (SWAT) team, organized as a division of the Special Operations Section under the jurisdiction of the Field Operations Division directed by Bobby J. Rocker. The deployment of the SWAT team members, protected by heavy, bulletproof shields and safety gear, stopped the massacre perpetrated by Burton, who, when he realized that he was surrounded, committed suicide.

Personal gear
Often much of the officer's personal gear is carried on the belt, including a double magazine carrier, a pepper spray holster, the fixtures of the leg holster and the rappelling harness used in some assault missions

THE SPECIAL OPERATIONS SECTION OF ATLANTA

Prepared for action

This operation, along with the many others they must carry out to respond to the fifty or so annual calls they have, was conducted by the fifteen men and women –there is a woman who is a sniper– who constitute the SWAT assault unit, commanded by a lieutenant and consisting of two squadrons directed by sergeants.

Their professional skill has grown since the unit was created in 1972 to fight crime, and today, after it was restructured in 1975 to have 25 members, the SWAT team consists of a compact unit in which the specialization of the team prevails over individuality, so that all members can carry out the most varied tasks, although among

Modern arms
The Special Weapons And Tactics Team of the Atlanta Police Department use modern weapons that include Colt SMG submachine guns, which fire 9x19 millimeter Parabellum caliber bullets and are equipped with sophisticated aiming devices.

their ranks are three individuals specialized as snipers and six as bomb deactivation experts. This preparation has caused them to be chosen to cover the outer ring –the inner one is assigned to the Secret

Explosives experts
The Atlanta SWAT team. Among its most highly-trained personnel a bomb squad composed of professionals qualified to handle all types of explosive devices, a capacity which allows them to use bombs to support their partners or to deactivate terrorist bombs.

Service– that protects President Bill Clinton when he travels to their city, or to collaborate with the renowned SEAL (Sea, Air and Land) of the U.S. Navy to carry out training activities together.

Assault teams

The two basic elements of the Unit are its two squadrons, trained to carry out diverse police tasks: handling abductions and hostage situations, dealing with criminals entrenched in a building, protecting Very Important People who visit the city, provide rapid response in high risk situations, and arrest drug traffickers, operations which they have been carrying out since their inception without ever

THE SPECIAL OPERATIONS SECTION OF ATLANTA

Arrest
The arrest of this presumed drug trafficker is emphatic. The officer keeps him face down and applies the weight of his body while pointing a submachine gun at him, allowing him to handcuff the suspect to immobilize him.

having suffered a casualty in their ranks and having caused only four casualties among those who resisted.

As it is a small unit with experienced members, some of whom have been with the unit for more than 10 years of continuous service, very few vacancies become available, and when there is a space free, much is demanded of the aspiring candidates. Furthermore, they must have an excellent service record, worked for other police units for over five years, and have certain additional merits, such as having belonged to special military groups or have shooting instructor certification, characteristics which will help in selecting the most prepared candidates.

The candidates chosen for additional testing follow a month-long training course taught by their future colleagues, which serves to promote team spirit as well as teach them certain special techniques and work methods and introduce them to the material they will be using. If they pass this initial stage, they go on

Safe transport
When a package with explosives in it is detected, bomb experts place it, with the help of the robot, in this armor-plated container capable of withstanding very powerful explosions. Once inside the container, the bomb will be transported to a place where it can be detonated.

THE SPECIAL OPERATIONS SECTION OF ATLANTA

to take a course at the AFS (Advanced Firearms School), carried out at one of the several schools existing throughout the country to become qualified in the use of the most varied types of firearms and learn how to move or react when faced with diverse police scenarios.

Daily activity

When they return to the Unit, they join the squadrons as regular members and participate in the training that the Unit regularly carries out with similar national units and on their own premises as daily exercises. The latter is part of their regular workday -from 10am to 6pm- and includes physical fitness, shooting exercises in a firing range adjoining their premises, located in an area away from the center of the city, assault practice in the most varied locations -from high rises in the center of the city, to the metro within the metropolitan area- and practicing operations in the city's fire station tower. In these facilities, they practice rappel, climbing ladders, cleaning rooms and take advantage of the building to practice entries using tear gas or stun grenades.

This tower is also used to program activities in very concrete situations, as it allows them to exercise with a real fire that generates enough smoke such that

the team members are forced to wear gas masks that limit their field of vision, it allows them to practice simultaneous window entry by rappelling down the side of the building from the roof, or practice entry with explosives in inner rooms. These rooms do not have doors. A specially designed one is placed in their entrance to be blown off, at which point the assault squad makes a rapid, sweeping entrance.

These exercises, serving as a complement to their real missions, are supplemented by firing examinations which must be passed every six months, in which a minimum score is required, depending on the type of weapon and range. In addition, members must comply with specific requirements in order to continue on the team. Furthermore, the three individuals most qualified in precision shooting with long weapons go through the firing facilities every two weeks to test their capacity to repeatedly

Total camouflage
The Atlanta Police Department's snipers use ghillie suit-type outfits that allow them to blend into their surroundings when they operate in rural environments. In this manner the criminals cannot ascertain the point from which they are being shot at.

Deactivation
A heavy, Canadian-made, bombproof suit covers this bomb expert's entire body during the process of checking a suspicious package, an operation which he carries out with the help of a portable x-ray machine.

hit a target the size of an eye at a distance of 100 metros.

Explosives deactivators

The SWAT team in the State of Georgia has the greatest number of people specialized in handling and deactivating the most varied types of explosive devices, people who have studied at the Bomb School (BS) in Hansfield, Alabama, to train in this field along with other personnel from the Federal Bureau of Investigation (FBI) and the Armed Forces. They have namely three bomb experts and a sergeant assigned to the Airport Section to cover the city's enormous airport, that receives approximately forty-eight million passengers per year.

They are responsible for maintenance of operative equipment consisting of detection and neutralizing elements for use should a bomb be detected in one of the hundreds of thousands of suitcases moving through the airport, or in the packages sent by transportation companies. The other group of specialists, which

THE SPECIAL OPERATIONS SECTION OF ATLANTA

includes six more people, shares daily duties with the rest of SWAT team members and constitutes the operative support nucleus for entry with explosives. They deactivate explosive devices located in the city, where nearly half a million people live.

The equipment they have available consists of a robot with caterpillar traction –it can turn in order to move between the rows of seats of an airplane. Made by the American firm Remotec, it is remote-control operated, and called Boomer in reference to the enormous bubbles it blows when chewing the gum of the same name. This robot, which allows all sort of objects to be handled from a distance, is controlled from a console with a screen located in the back of a van. It has two daytime video cameras -one in black and white, the other in color- and another night vision camera to see in any light conditions, a laser attached to a shotgun used to break certain types of packages or detonate them, a flashlight to illuminate particularly dark areas, a disruptive

NIGHT STALKER LASER MODULE

Due to the increasingly sophisticated means used by criminals and to the fact that police operations must often be carried out in adverse conditions, the Atlanta Police Department has had to acquire modern equipment for its SWAT Unit, including the Night Stalker/SO/FL module manufactured by UITC Armament Corporation, based in Portsmouth, New Hampshire.
This device, similar to the one that US special forces employ in their Mk23 pistols, model 0, is attached to Colt SMG submachine guns, in the area designed for the attachment of a bayonet. The body includes a potent flashlight powered by a 3 volt lithium battery, a laser emitter that projects a 635 nanometer ray that is visible during the day, and another laser emitter projecting at 830 nm that's passive, emitting a ray that can only be seen when wearing night vision glasses or other appropriate means, very useful for preventing an assault group from detection. The module has a pistol grip near the bottom that allows the weapon to be held more comfortably, and activation buttons on its side.

THE SPECIAL OPERATIONS SECTION OF ATLANTA

cannon which ejects a jet of water at high pressure, and an articulated arm to pick up objects. A significant characteristic is that it is controlled via a roll of wire 1,000 meters long, thus preventing interference that could be caused by aircraft radio control equipment.

Members of the Atlanta Police Bomb Squadron, as they are known within the Department, travel in Chevrolet and Ford Econoline 350 and F350 vans, used to carry certain equipment and to haul the armor-plated container in which suspicious packages are deposited for transport to a detonation point. Their personal gear includes EOD-7B bombproof suits made by the Canadian firm Met-ENG Systems, protective shields and vests designed for transporting deactivation equipment, while general equipment includes wheelbarrows and x-ray scanners and developers, both portable.

Varied and modern equipment

In addition to specific deactivation equipment, there is a long list of elements used by the SWAT team in general in training and operations, ranging from plastic handcuffs for criminal arrests, to sophisticated armored vehicles used to reach high-risk areas without being disturbed by snipers nor perturbed individuals.

Special armaments

In contrast to other similar groups, the Atlanta SWAT team has adopted a weapon that is out of the norm and follow very specific requirements regarding its acquisition: economy, simplicity and perfect operation. For this reason, and although the Austrian firm Glock, whose productive plant is located in the same state, has offered them free pistols, they use the Smith & Wesson 5903 semiautomatic as a secondary weapon. Its features include: aluminum frame to reduce

Training
On the outskirts of Atlanta there is a training area for police officers and firefighters with a high rise for practicing assaults using rappel, or moving up staircases to reach the rooms where criminals would be located.

Entering
A group of officers, armed with Smith & Wesson 5903 semiautomatic pistols of 9x19 mm Parabellum caliber, enter a building in search of a suspect. This pistol is an emphatic weapon for handling lightly armed adversaries.

THE SPECIAL OPERATIONS SECTION OF ATLANTA

High risk situations
In those cases in which the suspects whom the police are trying to arrest do not desist, the officers may use tear gas cartridges or smoke grenades that are launched with a single-shot shotgun.

weight; slide with the Department's emblem, made of steel for greater strength; tritium sights for aiming in adverse light conditions; and stainless steel magazines which can hold up to 15, 9x19 millimeter Parabellum cartridges, and another that can be fed into the chamber.

Their basic assault weapon is the SMG 635, a curious submachine gun manufactured by the firm Colt, based on the M16 assault rifle but modified –shortened, generally made smaller and chambered to fit 20 to 32 cartridge magazines for 9 mm Parabellum. This weapon is compact and so simple to use that minimally trained people can handle it. It also features light weight –it weighs somewhat more than 2 1/2 kilograms– and has proven efficient, accurate, lacking interruptions and very stable in semiautomatic firing –shot per shot–, the mode in which these groups normally carry out their assaults. Another feature is its extensible buttstock to facilitate transport when no shooting is required.

To improve its performance, a C-More sight has been added, affixed to the

Firing range
Adjoining the Atlanta SWAT team's station is a large firing range where team members practice, in weekly shifts, in the use of assigned weapons against targets located at short and medium range.

THE SPECIAL OPERATIONS SECTION OF ATLANTA

AN/PVS-7B NIGHT VISION GOGGLES

The US firm ITT Defense, as well as other American companies, manufacture AN/PVS-7B night vision goggles for military and security force use. This model, along with models C, which is submergible, and D, upgraded in 1999, come with a headstrap to attach to the user's head when hands-free use is desired, and a vision module consisting of a front monocular with a third generation tube and a binocular that is attached directly in front of the user's eyes.

The kit includes an infrared emitter that provides vision in areas where the absence of light is total, has a lens protector and can be used for night movement as well as for surveillance of specific targets. The tube's life is approximately 7,500 hours, the module weighs 680 grams, does not include magnifying lenses, has a focus that adjusts from 25 centimeters to infinity and is powered by two 1.5 volt alkaline batteries or one lithium battery, and can be adjusted for eye width.

upper grip and including a screen with a point used as a reference; as well as a Night Stalker/SO/FL module, manufactured by UITC Armament Corporation, which significantly increases capacity for use in any circumstances, as it includes flashlight and lasers.

As complementary weapons, they use 5.56x45 mm caliber AR-15A1 assault rifles, which are based on the M16 but semiautomatic; Remington, 12-caliber, slide-operated shotguns, model 870 and 7.62x51 mm Remington M700 bolt-action rifles, equipped with a curious ITT 2.5-10x56 sight with a day sight channel and an optronic element for amplification of residual light allowing night time firing or firing in situations with particular absence of light.

In the previous weapons, to achieve improved performance for those police scenarios in which target neutralization must be done most rapidly and efficiently, ammunition used includes: 9 mm Winchester Silvertrip bullets with 147-grain, high-deformation tips; 12 Winchester loaded with 9 double zero pellets, both in their regular 12/70 version and in 12/76 Magnum; 5.56 (.223 Remington) in their military version with 55-grain armored tips as well as semi-armored high-deformation tips; and 7.62 (.308 Winchester) Gold Medal HPBT (Hollow Point Boat Tail) model, loaded with 168-grain tips designed to achieve remarkable accuracy and very good groups.

Conclusive
The Colt AR-15A1 assault rifles used in Atlanta are a semiautomatic modification of the M16 in which the capacity to fire in bursts has been eliminated, the fixed buttstock has been replaced with a retractile one, and a considerably large flashlight has been mounted to it.

THE SPECIAL OPERATIONS SECTION OF ATLANTA

Accuracy
This woman is one of the Unit's snipers. She combines her principle duties as a member of an assault group with training in the use of this accurate, .308 Winchester caliber, bolt-operated rifle.

Specialized accessories

SWAT team operations require the use of specific materials that improve their capacity and allow them to act in adverse conditions. This includes their personal gear as well as various systems used as support for group missions. The members of this SWAT team wear tactical or military combat boots, a light green body suit to facilitate movement, and a modern Safariland belt at the waist, and a rigid, synthetic holster attached to the calf. These elements have a variety of accessories for transporting additional magazines for pistols, handcuffs, communications equipment transmitters, pepper spray and ASP metallic batons.

Personal safety is insured through the use of helmets of two types –the PASGT model made of Kevlar used by the armed forces, and a helmet manufactured by the French firm GFS, made of Spectrashield–, bulletproof vests by the firm Progressive Technology capable of withstanding all sorts of impacts from small-caliber bullets, as they are Type IIIA. In situations of greatest risk, they place a TAC-4 ceramic plate in a large breast pocket in order to stop bullets fired from rifles.

Other gear they use in action include ITT AN/PSV-7B night vision glasses with third generation tubes, Motorola MX-2000 communications equipment connected to a converter that allows speaking into a microphone without having to hold anything in one's hands and Bell-Voice tracking devices to know officers' locations at all times. Snipers use Bushnell lasers to ascertain their exact distance from a target, as well as camouflage uniforms like ghillie suits, made by the firm U.S. Cavalry, which allow them to remain undetected in woodland areas in order to carry out their missions unobserved.

At times they must enter premises in which armed criminals are hiding. For this purpose, they use Omni Blast 1000 stun grenades, which produce a deafening sound and flashes of light upon detonation, momentarily blinding the opponent. It is also the norm to use 37 mm bullets loaded with CS tear gas, fired with a single-shot Federal Ordnance

Robot
At a distance, from inside a specially designed van, this robot, Boomer, is being controlled. It is equipped with various video cameras and an articulated arm that allows it to move with precision when packages suspected of containing explosives or bombs are found.

shotgun or with a pistol manufactured by S&W Chemical Corporation.

These weapons, as well as others loaded with rubber bullets used to break glass or knock down doors, are carried in special tactical vests, which can also carry smoke bombs used to hide officers' movements and make the adversary react more slowly. As complements, military gas masks are also used, with the filter in front. They are transported in bags that the officers normally attach to their sides such that they do not interfere when they are not being used.

And finally, they also have a large fleet of unmarked vehicles available, as well as some marked ones to indicate that the SWAT team is in the area, which can also cause the opponent that is to be neutralized to desist. The latter include Caprice cars used for transporting the officers in their

THE SPECIAL OPERATIONS SECTION OF ATLANTA

reconnaissance and patrol missions throughout the metropolitan area, regular vans for transporting the men to the point of action or deployment, and other vans with armor plating and cabinets as well as all sorts of fittings for carrying the equipment necessary in their operations, off road pick-ups for activities in rural areas or operations that require driving through steep areas or rough roads, armor-plated trucks for high-risk situations in which they could be shot at and in which the steel plating of the chassis can prove useful, and even ambulances to quickly transport any injured officer, be this during training exercises or in real deployment.

Remote control
The robot used by bomb deactivation specialists is controlled by a specialist from a console located in a van, who directs all its movements from a safe distance.

Coordinated movement
Assault groups must coordinate their action to insure greater efficiency and the safety of their members. For this reason, police officers train in all sorts of places and with a great variety of scenarios.

SPECIALIZED VEHICLES

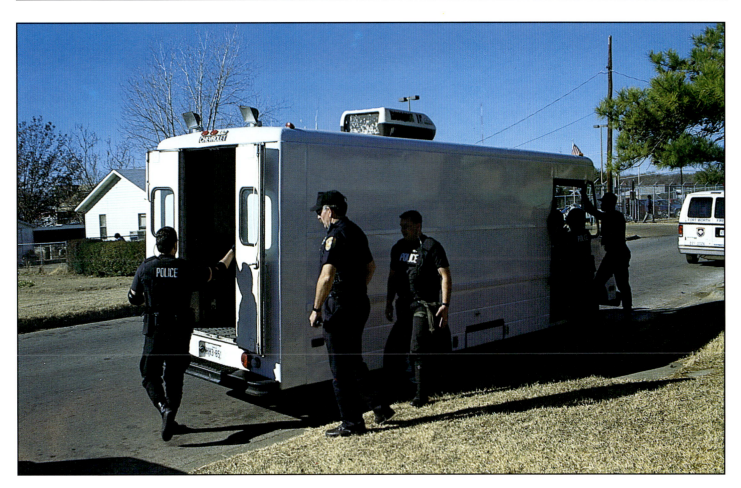

Just as other police units use a wide range of vehicles to carry out their daily activities, Law Enforcement Special Assault Groups make use of a wide range of models, from unmarked cars for daily travel to control vans from which high-risk operations are directed.

Although some of the vehicles mentioned are regular models acquired on the automobile market, a great deal of the vehicles used by this type of unit are specially designed for them or are models that have been customized to meet the specific requirements of the units. It is possible to find unique examples, created to meet detailed specifications, in the fleet of vehicles of an assault group.

Specific modifications
The Italian GIS have modified their Range Rovers, adding supports on which they place extensible ladders for access to high places during assault missions, especially to aircraft fuselage.

High risk assault
To carry out this type of operations, various vehicle models are used to provide support for assault action, both providing mobility to assault teams and protection for their advance. They can also be used to transport the team to the point at which operations are to be commenced.

Arrest of criminals
The members of the Fort Worth SWAT team in Texas used this van to travel to the place where they commenced an assault on a home in which drugs were sold. The vehicle is unmarked so that the officers can go undetected.

SPECIALIZED VEHICLES

Customized modifications

The missions assigned to Law Enforcement Special Units include handling hostage situations in aircraft, on ships or on land, as well as operations against terrorist groups, which require very peculiar materials. To gain access to elevated locations such as the fuselage of passenger aircraft and apartments at least ten meters from the ground, or to achieve a favorable situation with respect to the adversary, recourse is made to customized vehicles, the result of modifying commercial off-road trucks.

The Spanish GEO special unit, for example, use long Patrol off-road vehicles, with a platform installed over the roof on which to affix ladders of diverse lengths, thus facilitating the speed at which officers can begin a climb to reach the established objective. A similar model is used by the Italian GIS unit, which has transformed a Range Rover by attaching extensible ladders to one of the sides, or the Czech URNA officers, who use US Cherokees on which they have attached bars on the lower and upper parts of the chassis: officers climb onto the lower bars while holding onto the upper ones, so that they can intervene more readily should the situation require.

In Europe, this type of modification is quite common. Thus, the Norwegian Beredskapstroppen often use Mercedes

and Chevrolet Blazer off-road vehicles with modifications on the upper part of the chassis, while the Portuguese Grupo de Operaçoes Especiais use Range Rovers, modified in the same manner.

Armor-plated protection

Among the equipment used by these units are cars modified to withstand the impact of bullets fired from light weapons or of small explosive devices. These vehicles are often deployed in high-risk areas, including detachments protecting diplomatic legations in countries involved in civil wars or considerable disturbances. They can be used on missions to protect VIPs, and they can play a significant role in the arrest of very dangerous criminals. Some German, high-horsepower Mercedes, such as the GSG9, even have a port in the windshield so that officers can fire weapons from inside.

Armor-plating depends on the unit's specific needs and on the funding approved for its acquisition, the most common armor being able to withstand impacts from bullets of up to 7.62 millimeter cali-

Protection services
Motorcycles, both the high-power road motorcycles as well as the off-road bikes, can be used as support vehicles for special police units. One of the activities for which they are used are for rapid escort missions for VIPs.

Total protection
This Phoenix police team uses an armored vehicle in high risk situations in which opponent fire is foreseen. When the officers get out, they protect themselves with heavy bullet-proof shields.

ber, and even shrapnel caused by grenades thrown at them. Even stronger and more specialized are some armored light vehicles assigned to police units in the United States, a country in which greater protection is needed for assaults due to the proliferation of the use of firearms among criminals.

Among the most significant vehicles are customized vans, armor-plated for military use and acquired from Army overstocks, or specially manufactured models. Some of the best models currently in use are the Peace-Keepers assigned to the Emergency Response Team of the Washington Police Department, which has three of these armor-plated vehicles on hand, to the Tactical Response Team of Kansas, to the Special Weapons and Tactics Team of Atlanta, and to the Special Response Team of Phoenix, to name just a few.

A very effective modified vehicle is the BART (Bureau Armored Rescue Truck) used by the Special Emergency Reaction Team of Portland. This truck is

SPECIALIZED VEHICLES

very similar to, and probably based on, vehicles designed for transporting money from banks. Remarkable features of its design are the rear platform, where up to five officers can position themselves, ready to jump into action, its two side doors that can be opened to provide additional protection, and the shooting slits located in the sides of the vehicles.

Even more powerful are the Cadillac Gage V-100 4x4 used by the Kansas TRT, the armored Mowag Piranhas with six-wheel drive used by the Swiss Flughafenpolizei Sicherheitsabteilung Einsatzgrup-

Military origin
The Atlanta Police Department uses various armored vehicles granted by the military or donated by civilians. Thanks to their armor plating, these allow them to safely reach dangerous areas where shootings or serious incidents have occurred.

pen (FLUSIPO), which are often used at major airports, or the ERV (Emergency Rescue Vehicle) with caterpillar tracks, of military origin and used by the New York Police Department.

Equipment transport
US tactical intervention groups often use vans such as the one in the photograph to transport collective support equipment, some special weapons and other elements necessary for carrying out their missions.

Total mobility

The need to arrive more quickly at the point where an operation is to commence, the need for their movements to be discrete in order not to arouse suspicion in the case of operations against terrorist groups and the restrictions on the immediate use of aircraft have caused the creation of a wide range of originally commercial vehicles modified by specialized companies or following specific customer specifications, to meet the needs of: speed, low vulnerability, adaptation and effectiveness for special police operations.

SPECIALIZED VEHICLES

Total discretion
To facilitate the arrival of special officers to the site of a mission, automobiles with high-power engines are often used to allow for high velocity. They carry groups of up to four officers, with their weapons and personal gear in the trunk.

Materials transport

When a police assault team takes action outside of its operative base, it often needs support material to allow it to train or work for a period of several days. Light vans are used for this, as well as heavy vans and even trucks of a variety of sizes, often with the addition of a trailer.

With the exception of specific models, such as the diving support vehicles carrying all sorts of diving equipment or the trucks for transporting various types of ladders used by the Spanish GEO unit, this type of vehicles is quite common among special police units throughout the world, who use them regularly. Famous examples are the vans used by the Emergency Service Unit of the New York Police Department, which travel the streets of this metropolis, providing mobility for the special team and transportation for the materials required for special operations. Their presence is enough to let the population and criminals know that the ESU team is in the vicinity, prepared to take action should their uniformed colleagues need their help or should the situation call for it.

Similar modifications are carried out on vehicles in many other places to transport their equipment. These basically consist of a container located in the rear area or in a specially designed armored area in the loading zone, with various compartments holding: materials for opening doors or gates, such as metal sheers, sledge hammers or jimmies; collective

SOLID TIRES

Several companies in the world manufacture bulletproof tires that cannot be perforated, sometimes used on special police group assault squad vehicles. These models have the advantage of incorporating a solid material inside, as in the photograph of the French Michelin/Hutchinson tire, to prevent a bullet or sharp object from perforating them and making them lose their capacity to roll and thus jeopardize a mission.
The internal structure of these tires allows them to travel hundreds of kilometers at high speeds, even when they have been hit by bullets or grenade shrapnel, being very useful accessories for armored or assault vehicles. Nonetheless, their use is not yet very widespread, because they are expensive and require special care in order to maintain their characteristics and the elasticity of their materials.

SPECIALIZED VEHICLES

protective gear, such as shields of various sizes; powerful systems for knocking down doors including battering rams of various weights and sizes; auxiliary lighting sets consisting of portable searchlights and mobile generators; listening and observation sets with directional microphones, video cameras or nocturnal surveillance equipment; ladders, poles, ropes and other means that allow them to reach areas difficult to access; various types of explosives, detonators and string for blasting open doors or windows previous to assault; special weapons such as shotguns or precision rifles; bulletproof vests with ceramic plates for situations of greater risk; communications equipment to maintain communication with command centers and, if necessary, with the criminals; and a wide range of other equipment, including objects for specific missions or the needs foreseen for the area of deployment.

They also often transport other elements, normally in air-tight containers or protective bags, such as smoke grenade launchers and various devices that can be shot with them, gas masks, tactical and ghillie suit-type uniforms for snipers, various and special ammunition, emergency food rations to allow them total autonomy on the job, and refrigerators

Rapid assault
The Spanish GEO team uses several modified, off-road, long Patrol vehicles with a roof structure that allows the installation of ladders of variable lengths, depending on the need, with which to reach difficult areas more quickly.

for storing a variety of refreshing drinks, a very common habit in the US teams, whose officers demonstrate a great need for continuous hydration.

General support
Among the fleet used by these units are high-power motorcycles to protect convoys travelling along the highway, off-road motorcycles for access to rough terrain, all sorts of automobiles for surveillance activities, tailing or daily travel, and vans for transporting the team to the place of action.

Busses of various sizes are also used for those situations requiring the transportation of special contingents, or trucks, such as those used by the SRT of the Miami Metro Dade Police, that have been equipped with very strong fenders and are used to knock down doors or walls while the officers remain in the rear

of the vehicle, holding on to metallic bars located on the sides and ready to take action.

Also specialized are trailers modified as mobile command centers, among which are some large trailers deployed by the Phoenix and Chicago Police Departments, called HBT Mobile Command Post/Negotiation Point, which has wide work space, computers and air conditioning, among other features. Also noteworthy are the Belgian Gendarmerieeinsatzkommando Cobra's Steyr 4x4 trucks, equipped with generators and lighting systems, off-road vehicles designed for towing trailers with heavy equipment such as rubber dinghies and outboard motors, or vehicles designed for police use, such as the American Crown Victoria, the French Citroën XM and Peugeot 405 MI16, and the German Mercedes Benz 300SE.

Total mobility
The members of the Czech URNA unit have been assigned American Cherokees powered by motors with 4-liter gas tanks and modified with elements on the outside which the officers can hold on to for quick transport.

SPECIALIZED VEHICLES

Command center
Many police departments have vehicles specially designed for command and control tasks. They are equipped with built-in presentation tables, viewing screens and communications equipment that allow the most varied operations to be coordinated.

Tactical requirements
The SWAT Team in Scottsdale, Arizona employs this enormous van as support for training exercises and missions. Inside, it is carrying a variety of equipment, from searchlights with portable generators to ammunition with high perforation capacity.

CZECH SPECIAL POLICE

Training
URNA officers train continuously in various simulated scenarios, including the rapid detainment of a vehicle in which dangerous individuals suspected of having committed some crime are travelling, as can be observed here.

The Czech Republic is a country that arose as a consequence of the division of former Czechoslovakia, which was the union of two ethnic groups, the Czechs and the Slovaks. The adaptation of this country to Western standards of living, and especially to the military and social structures that characterize the development of present-day Europe, has given rise to the appearance of new threats to society, such as terrorist groups, organized crime and a great variety of Mafias.

To handle these threats, an antiterrorist unit is kept on call which is known by the Czech name of Utvar rychleho nasazeni, although among similar groups in the West that maintain contacts with them they are known by the acronym of URNA.

Facilities
The URNA is quartered approximately seventy-five kilometers from Prague in facilities that include buildings for officers to practice indoor maneuvers, moving through corridors and up staircases to improve coordination of team movements.

CZECH SPECIAL POLICE

Selected from among the best
To achieve a cohesive and homogenous group with regard to capacity and preparation, a rigorous selection and training process is followed which allows the selection of the most appropriate officers for this type of operations, for which it is as important to have sound emotional stability as to be qualified for the diverse activities at hand.

Specific prerequisites
All those who want to become members of the URNA must take the tests given at variable times to cover available spaces when officers move on to other units. The candidates must also meet specific prerequisites. They must: be at least 23 years old, have completed the Police Corps' basic training and qualification program and have served in the Corps for at least 3 years, present accreditation of secondary or higher level studies, have a driver's license for regular motor vehicle driving, meet certain concrete require-

Travel
Jeep Cherokee off-road vehicles allow them to arrive rapidly at places where training is held or real operations are to begin. These jeeps are also modified to act as support for their assault or protective missions.

Assault
The risk of an incident occurring in an aircraft hijacking situation with hostages is very high. For this reason, URNA officers train in various assault techniques with specific equipment, such as these ladders that allow them to reach the hatches of the aircraft.

ments regarding swimming skills, be in good health and have outstanding physical ability.

Once candidates have demonstrated that they meet these requirements, a group is selected to follow a validation program with three eliminatory stages, such that those who don't pass the first stage cannot go on to the second and so forth. The evaluators are URNA members and have gained a great deal of experience during their many years of service. The first stage includes a very complex medical examination with the aim of ascertaining each individual's limits for withstanding extreme physical strain under the most varied conditions of effort and endurance, complemented by a written examination to ascertain the person's psychological profile in such aspects as resistance to stress, capacity for adaptation, tolerance to teamwork, intelligence and flexibility to carry out diverse tasks.

Those who pass these first two test move on to the third stage, which will demonstrate which candidates are physically most apt. They run a 60 meter race, they are timed for running 5 kilometers and tested on their capacity for doing sit-ups and pushups in a specific period of time, their are clocked swimming a distance of 400 meters, they must climb a rope 4.5 meters long, and finally, they run an obstacle course.

The previous tests allow the candidates to be narrowed down to a small group which goes on to the second stage. This includes some tests during a week of hard and continuous work seeking to ascertain aspects such as the capacity to endure physical and psychological tests, their resistance to fatigue and exhaustion, their capacity to withstand continuous stress for long periods of time and to make decisions at critical moments, and their courage and capacity for teamwork.

The candidates must complete marches carrying heavy backpacks, carry out individual or team maneuvers and some sort of group work. Each activity is controlled and has a time limit that the recruits, naturally, do not know. The evaluators monitor them closely. Passing this part of the selection process generally depends on each indivi-

CZECH SPECIAL POLICE

dual's capacity to maintain the appropriate level of decisiveness, motivation, imagination and endurance.

The best among them will have to pass a third stage, in which they are personally interviewed by the commander of the Unit, who asks the candidates why they were interested in becoming a member of the team. This personal contact allows the evaluators to make a more precise decision in choosing candidates.

After this, those selected undergo a process of preparation in various areas that lasts several months and which not

Sniper
The snipers of this Czech Unit are equipped with Swiss SSG 3000 bolt-action rifles, weapons that fire .308 Winchester caliber ammunition with great precision, whether by day or by night.

everyone passes. After receiving their personal qualification, they become part of the group and participate in collective tasks and exercises to slowly get used to carrying out the antiterrorist tasks assigned the Unit. These tasks they will have to combine with support tasks in high-risk arrests requested by the Division Handling Organized Crime or the Antidrug Brigade of the Czech Police.

The core of their daily training activities consist of tactical procedures necessary for carrying out assaults on aircraft, buildings, trains, buses or metros. The rest of training is oriented towards arrest procedures, high level escorts and protection of VIPs. A fact worth mentioning is that all of the members of operative units are qualified as paratroopers using manually opening parachutes.

Western equipment
Personal gear includes Midnite boots in Gore-Tex by the US firm HI-TEC, and

CZECH SPECIAL POLICE

Puma boots, dark blue body suit made of a combination of Nomex and Gore-Tex to facilitate transpiration and to provide water-tightness, face mask, tactical jacket, leg holster for a pistol and stun grenades, as well as camouflage uniforms used by snipers. On the front of the jackets there is a large reflective emblem identifying them as members of the Police Force.

The officer's personal gear is very complete. For this reason they have tactical goggles manufactured by the French firm Bollé to protect their eyes from small impacts during entries using explosives or from very small bullets, light bulletproof vests by the Irish firm High Mark and the US firm Point Blank, heavy bulletproof vests by High Mark, Combat ballistic helmets without facial protection made by the German company Schubert, and Titan helmets with a armored visor made by the Swiss company Tip Bicord. They cover their movements with heavy bulletproof shields manufactured in Britain by the firm Bristol.

Their personal gear principally consists of elements acquired from the most reputed Western manufacturers, with a small percentage acquired from national

companies. For assaults, they use the MP5 range of submachine guns manufactured by the German company Heckler und Koch, weapons that fire ammunition of 9x19 millimeter Parabellum caliber made by various manufacturers, among which are frangible cartridges and red markers by the Canadian firm SIMUNITION, armored bullets with tips of 7.5 and 8.5 grams by the Czech company Sellier Bellot, those manufactured by Mag Tech in Brazil and the US 3D type bullets.

This range of ammunition is normally used in magazines holding 30 cartridges that feed into the MP5, of which they use the KA4 variant, compact and equipped

Equipment
URNA members have modern equipment principally manufactured in Europe, with outstanding garments and protective gear and very sophisticated armaments.

Training
The tire house is a building with movable parts on wheels to simulate buildings for training purposes. The interior can be quickly modified to simulate the specific types of buildings in which real assaults must be carried out.

with a selector for three positions, the A5 with metallic, retractable buttstock and the option of choosing controlled bursts of fire, and the SD6, which stands out for its long silencer built into the barrel of the weapon, an element that decreases the noise level caused by detonation so that it becomes more discrete. These weapons are normally equipped with 4-power optical sights placed on a specific H&K mount and many of them also have flashlights and laser sights.

It is also possible to use the above-mentioned 9 mm cartridges with the regulation pistol, corresponding to models 75 and 85 by the Czech firm Ceská Zbrojov-

CZECH SPECIAL POLICE

ka, weapons that stand out for their toughness, good grip, double-action firing system and cartridges that hold 15 bullets. These secondary weapons are used for their reliability and durability rather than superior quality, especially considering that operation or assault are not normally carried out solely with pistols.

The Italian manual slide-operated Astra Franci shotguns, or the manual, dual-action or semiautomatic Benelli M3Ts, also made in Italy, are more powerful due to the 12 caliber bullets they fire. They take various types of ammunition, including diverse models of

Simultaneous
While one group of officers remains crouched at the front of the aircraft, a second team moves toward the port side, and another one is positioned at the starboard side. At the command, they will simultaneously enter through the hatches to neutralize the hijackers inside the aircraft.

Sellier Bellot loaded with bullets and that range in length from 12/65 to 12/76 Magnum types. They also use those loaded with high kinetic energy bullets designed to blast locks and bolts on doors in apartments and buildings under assault.

In high precision tasks, the famous bolt-action rifles made by the Swiss firm Sig Sauer are used, namely model 3000, which features chambering for the use of 7.62x51 mm (.308 Winchester) cartridges, that are capable of reaching targets within a range of 600 meters. This weapon also has a very ergonomic and fully adjustable buttstock, a 24 inch barrel that

VARIOUS EXPLOSIVE DEVICES

Used by the URNA members as support elements for their assault operations. Some of the more significant among these are P1 stun grenades (on the right) which, when thrown in an enclosed space, generally a small room, produce several very strong detonations combined with many intense flashes of light that disorient the people inside, causing a moment of confusion that the assault team uses to enter the room.
They also use P2 grenades (red in color), which when the safety pin is removed and they are thrown, emit a great deal of CS tear gas, causing a great deal of eye irritation, symptoms of choking and coughing attacks in those who inhale the gas, limiting their capacity to react. And finally, they also use smoke bombs (on the left) that can be used both to signal a landing place to aircraft supporting the assault group, and for throwing inside an enclosed area to prevent the people inside from seeing where the officers are coming from. The officers normally wear gas masks with filtering cartridges to protect themselves from the smoke or gas, protective earphones with integrated communications elements and safety goggles over their eyes.

CZECH SPECIAL POLICE

Assault
A group of four officers prepare to assault a house during an exercise, taking up positions that will allow two of them to enter rapidly while they are covered by their partners outside.

allows for high precision, and a sight base on which various sights can be mounted for day or night firing. Among the latter, one of the best is the Norwegian system KN202 made by Simrad Optronics, that can be coupled to the optical sight to allow aiming at night. Some of the cartridges used with this model are the Sniper model by the Swedish firm Norma and by Sellier Bellot, and the subsonic cartridge by the Finnish firm SAKO, optimized for use with a silencer that is screwed onto the muzzle of the rifle.

For assaults, they also use nationally manufactured plastic explosives, various types of detonators, detonating string of various gauges and Czech grenades that include the P1, a sort of stun grenade that produces detonations and flashes of light, and the P2, that emits CS tear gas produ-

cing a degree of paralysis in those who inhale it. As transport and assault vehicle, they use Jeep Cherokees that have been modified to meet their special needs. They often train with BO-105, Bell 412 and Mil Mi-8 helicopters as well.

Created at the beginning of the eighties

Under the auspices of the socialist government that governed Czechoslovakia, it was decided to establish a police unit consisting of specially trained and equipped officers in order to handle various threats with rapid action for which the military units that they had been relying on were not prepared.

Many settings
Their modern MP5A5 submachine guns include a selector that allows them to be fired in semiautomatic mode, or in controlled and free bursts, with a flashlight and laser sight module built into the handguard.

CZECH SPECIAL POLICE

Establishment

After initial work on certain significant aspects of their organization and assignment in 1980, it was decided to go ahead and create this rapid response Unit as a component of a larger police directorate that received the designation of 13th Directorate, being assigned to fight against all forms of crime, whether extraordinary or specific.

From 1981 to 1985, an ample officer training program was developed and the process of acquiring modern equipment and materials began. In this period, they demonstrated their great skill in various interventions in which terrorists were captured and various criminals were detained in high-risk operations. Special mention should be given to their operation to rescue two hostages being held in a country house in a vacation area by a subject who was seeking a ransom.

After this initial period, in which numerous operations were conducted, it was decided to reorganize the Unit to increase their duties to cover participation as a security force during riots and public protests, which led to a change in their name. This decision had a very negative impact on the Unit, as it began to be used by the Government of that time to repress protests carried out by increasingly numerous groups of civilians, who were made to desist using violent methods. Especially relevant were operations carried out between 1988 and 1989 against all sorts of popular revolts.

The change in political orientation that the country underwent caused the decision in February of 1990 to return the URNA to its original duties, and in the same year, they rescued a hostage held by a deranged individual wielding a hand grenade to prevent police action. They took rapid action to neutralize the individual and prevent him from hurting anyone.

Apart from smaller operations, some of the most significant actions on their record are the arrest in 1995 of a Russian Mafia head in a nightclub in Prague, the detention and dissolution of a Bulgarian Mafia group dedicated to drug and arms trafficking and to the control of prostitution establishments, as well as the capture of a leader of the Albanian Mafia who had established himself in the Czech Republic and for whom there was an international order of arrest requested by the Norwegian Police through Interpol.

Their activities against all sorts of crime are complemented by participation in police-oriented exercises, seminars and training sessions with other similar units from other countries. Their contacts have led them to share experiences with officers of the British 22 Special Air Service (SAS), various French and Italian

Camouflaged
Because URNA members must move through the most varied settings, they are trained to work in both urban as well as rural areas.

CZECH SPECIAL POLICE

units, members of the Swedish CTU and the Belgian SIE, and with the police officers of the Spanish Grupo de Operaciones Especiales (GEO).

Peculiar organizational structure

The principle mission of the Utvar rychleho nasazeni is to intervene against terrorists, abductors, hijackers and participate in high-risk assaults against suspects involved in criminal acts or drug trafficking within organized crime groups. To carry out these missions, it was decided to provide the URNA, which is under the direct authority of the Chief of Police and can only take action when authorized by the Minister of the Interior, with three basic elements of action res-

Illumination
MP5 submachine guns incorporate a potent Sure-Fire flashlight from the US, an element with a great deal of lighting capacity which allows clear vision in those areas where the absence of light makes it difficult to detect the adversary.

pectively in charge of general tasks, special services and assault missions, an operative structure which involves 110 people.

Power
The simultaneous entry of 4 men armed with MP5A5 and MP5SD6 submachine guns allows several suspects to be covered at once, with the certainty that they will hit by shots fired by the members of the assault group should they resist arrest or attempt to use their weapons.

The first of these divisions is a general administrative body, under the authority of the lieutenant colonel who acts as commander and takes care of administrative tasks through secretarial staff, chauffeurs, legal support personnel, etc. They carry out tasks related to the paperwork inherent in regular activity, and also take on logistics functions that include equipment maintenance, vehicle preparation to insure their readiness for use in programmed activities, materials management, handling of the arms and ammunition necessary for training, and an infinity of other general activities.

The second organizational division

CZECH SPECIAL POLICE

CZ PISTOL, MODEL 75

This semiautomatic manufactured by Ceská Zbrojovka at its Czech Republic plant, that in the past was made by BRNO, is a model manufactured entirely in steel and stands out for its excellent ergonomics, allowing it to adapt very well to the marksman's hand, for its sturdiness, allowing it to withstand the roughest treatment, and for the fact that its firing mechanism allows the user to choose between single and double-action modes.
It weighs one kilogram with an empty cartridge, measures 203 mm and is 22 mm wide, with a striated barrel 120 mm in length. It takes magazines with a capacity for 15 cartridges, plus the one that can be loaded into the chamber with total safety. The sights are built into the slide and have a 16 centimeter radius. Its rounded guard allows it to be easily picked up with both hands. This weapon is also made in a variant that fires in bursts, and an optimized model known as the CZ 85, although the snipers prefer the initial model as it is more robust.

consists of what is defined as special services and includes: the snipers in charge of using special rifles, who can achieve especially small groups and are capable of neutralizing a criminal or terrorist that is within range in a single shot; the specialists in charge of using sophisticated communications equipment that allows the Unit to communicate among its different elements and facilitates communication with superior command echelons; the personnel in charge of managing personal documentation and documentation relative to the various objectives and the general types of missions that they may have to undertake; and the negotiators qualified to maintain dialogue with individuals who are holding people hostage to ascertain their intentions and detect which would be the most appropriate moment to program a neutralization attempt.

The third is the most important, as it comprises a group of eighty-five or so police officers, although they could not carry out their duties without the support of the other two. It is the operations group and consists of three assault teams whose basic mission is to carry out high-

CZECH SPECIAL POLICE

Silenced
The MP5SD6 is a submachine gun equipped with an integrated silencer that is often used in conjunction with an optical sight for aiming against targets at a range of approximately 100 meters, obtaining remarkable effectiveness, even more so considering the limited power of 9x19 millimeter cartridges.

risk arrests requiring cohesive groups familiar with special techniques, teams that include both assault specialists and experts in all sorts of entries using mechanical methods as well as a variety of explosives.

The five people who specialize in handling explosive devices comprise what is known as the EOD (Explosive Ordnance Detail). They are also trained in scuba diving techniques so that they can carry out various underwater missions in which they use both skin diving techniques as well as scuba diving methods with air tanks, either single or double compressed air tanks, or with closed circuit oxygen equipment that does not emit air bubbles to prevent the frogmen's presence from being detected.

This entire human resources team is completely dedicated to their daily work, including the most complicated training exercises and regular shooting practice.

These usually take place in special facilities located at seventy-five kilometers or so from Prague which have buildings equipped with classrooms, shooting galleries, stock rooms, vehicle parking, etc., and a tire house, which is an assault practice facility with walls, rooms, hallways, etc., equipped with wheels so that structures can easily be changed depending on needs.

They also carry out training in other locations in their country, where they practice with all sorts of aircraft, on trains and metros, with a variety of platforms including state line coaches and in rural environments, normally supported by helicopters in their assaults.

Detention
This image accurately reflects how conclusive this arrest is, in which an officer maintains a criminal against the ground with the weight of his body, thus preventing him from reacting while he immobilizes the individual's hands with a strong element such as handcuffs or a nylon strap.

HECKLER UND KÖCH SUBMACHINE GUNS

The majority of police assault groups throughout the world rely on the German firm Heckler und Koch (H&K), which manufactures pistols, submachine guns, and different types of rifles of great quality and reliability. Their products, especially their MP5 submachine gun line, have attained great prestige for the variety of their offer, their aptness for criminal arrest or neutralization activities, and their availability in different configurations using diverse types of ammunition.

After its consolidation on the growing world market, promoted after the firm was acquired by the British group called Royal Ordnance, a plan for future growth has been established which includes the design and introduction of new products to increase their offer and meet the requirements that are foreseen to arise over the next few years..

Winning policy

This program is in keeping with their new line, presented towards the end of 1999 and including the model called PDW, or Personal Defense Weapon, which has no equivalent within established categories, as it is halfway between a pistol, a submachine gun and an assault rifle, similar to the former in size, to the second in rate of fire, and to the latter in firing power.

Interesting characteristics
Interesting features of the prototype presented at the AUSA Fair in the US and the MILIPOL Fair in France are its compact shape and its wide possibility for use. It is manufactured of various materials, among which is plastic polymer, which reduces its weight and lowers mass production costs.

This model is designed with the intention of meeting the needs of special police and military units, although it

Mini submachine gun
The K is a submachine gun in the MP5 line which is characterized by its ultra-compact size, which allows it to be concealed under a jacket or in a briefcase. Despite this, the weapon is capable of firing at rates of nearly two thousand rounds per minute.

Instinctive firing
Among the most significant features of the PDW is the front handguard, which can be folded out to allow the weapon to be held with the left hand as well and thus improve stability in instinctive aiming against short-range targets.

HECKLER UND KÖCH SUBMACHINE GUNS

Designed with plastic
H&K's PDWs make extensive use of plastic materials and weigh approximately 1.6 kilograms. Interesting features are the extendable buttstock to facilitate aiming, the handle on the handguard and the magazines that fit in the grip.

can also be used for such activities as protective or escort missions. For this reason, and in search of penetration power capable of perforating the bulletproof vests that are increasingly used by criminals and terrorists, a new 4.6x30 millimeter cartridge has been designed at their British factory in Radway Green. It combines a metallic casing with a steel bullet coated with metal to prevent rebound caused by its high velocity and little weight.

Regarding the latter characteristic, the bullet weighs 1.7 grams, is fired at an initial speed of 725 meters per second, with a kinetic energy of 447 joules. It can penetrate a sheet of titanium 1.6 mm thick coated with 20 layers of Kevlar at a range of 50 meters.

The weapon itself includes a selector for choosing between safety position, single shot mode or free burst mode. It is equipped with a front grip that can be folded out to facilitate instinctive shots with both hands. Its length when folded is 34 centimeters, with the additional length of the buttstock when it is extended to achieve better precision. Its 1.6 kilogram weight allows it to be carried comfortably, and its 20 or 40-cartridge magazines fit inside the handguard, providing the sufficient firepower required by its possible users. It fires at a rate of approximately nine hundred and fifty rounds per minute.

It has a gas-operated mechanism, the lock has a rotating head and the mounting lever, activated in order to feed the first cartridge from the magazine into the chamber, is located on the upper butt end. For aiming, it comes with an upper, reflex sight that is installed during the manufacturing process, which aids during instinctive firing with both hands or when it is rested on the left shoulder. In an emergency, conventional metallic

Training
The MP5A5PT is a variant that is specifically designed for training, as it fires cartridges with plastic bullets that cause no harm when fired from a certain distance. It has a blue sign on its frame to identify it vis-à-vis other weapons.

HECKLER UND KÖCH SUBMACHINE GUNS

sights located over the barrel can be used.

Improved products

Towards the end of 1998, the UMP45 (Universal Machine Pistol) program was also presented and subsequently put into production, after evaluating other projects, among were the MP5-PIP (Product Improved) and the MP2000, a submachine gun that stands out for its frame, made of plastic derivatives, and for shooting the potent .45 ACP cartridge that Americans like so much.

The weapon, which is also produced in a civilian variant that functions in semiautomatic mode and includes a long barrel in keeping with this use, stands out for its advanced characteristics. In the first place is weight, only 2.1 kg without the cartridge, due to the use of plastic polymers in all of its components, except elements such as the lock, barrel and small parts, which are made of steel. Despite its light weight, it is very stable in quick firing due to the low initial velocity of the bullet that it fires and to its design, which has improved its characteristics of re-elevation and ergonomics that facilitate accurate aiming.

Another interesting detail is its excellent performance, as it has been designed for a minimum life of approximately 100,000 shots. It is also designed to be disassembled in any situation, done by extracting its only pin. It is also significantly compact, which makes it easier to carry and quicker to put into place in order to fire, also due to the placement of its buttstock, which can be folded onto one side and includes a rubber pad to reduce the recoil against the shoulder of the user.

Plastic
To reach the low weight of little more than two kilograms for the UMP-45, plastic polymer derivatives have been used in all the parts possible, while the mechanism body, the magazine and a good deal of the inner parts are made of synthetic materials.

Other details that are remarkable in this design are the upper rail that allows various types of sights to be mounted to complement the fixed sights that come with the weapon; the possibility of affixing a silencer to the muzzle, which is very effective in combination with the .45 ACP bullets; the precision resulting from including a cold-forged, polygonal barrel, chromed on its inner rifling; and the advantage of a selector with which to choose among semiautomatic mode, double shot bursts, and free bursts.

The handguard includes standardized rails on which aiming sights can be affixed, or flashlights, pistol grips and other accessories. The weapon has other remarkable characteristics as well, such as: rate of fire of 580 rounds per minute with M1911 cartridges, and 700 with +P type cartridges, magazines with a capacity for 10 to 25 rounds, a total length of

Retractable buttstock
The UMP-45 is equipped with a retractile buttstock which allows it to become considerably smaller. The folded mode is used for firing instinctively against short-range targets, while it is extended for firing at longer-range targets.

HECKLER UND KÖCH SUBMACHINE GUNS

69 cm with the buttstock extended, and 45 cm when it is folded, a radius between sights of 325 mm and the incorporation of a MIL-STD-1913 rail on which various complements and accessories can be mounted.

Varied range

The MP5 line was the result of the adaptation of the G3 assault rifle so that it could fire a 9 mm Parabellum cartridge, a modification which required changes in the barrel, breechblock, cartridge rim and the butt, to name some of the most significant.

Conditions for use

Its older version, the MP5 submachine gun (Maschinen Pistole Fünf), demonstrated since its creation in 1964 that it was ideal as a light and effective weapon that maintained good effectiveness against targets at short and medium range, where the ammunition for which it was designed is effective.

The original model was quickly improved with small details that made it more ergonomic and improved its precision, and at the beginning of the 70s, modernized units were introduced with mounts on the upper part of the barrel to allow the attachment of various models of bases for vision and aiming sights.

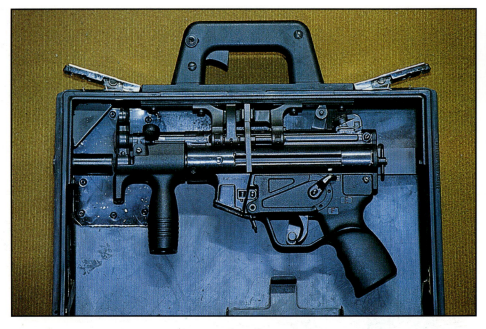

Among the initial versions was a model with fixed butt made of synthetic material that was called A2, and a variant equipped with retractile metallic buttstock known as A3, which is more compact as the buttstock is only unfolded for firing in cases in which the greatest precision is sought.

The latter characteristic is significant in these type of weapons, despite the short length of the barrel, as it allows groups of 20 cm when firing at a range of 100 meters. The success of sales led to the creation of optimized versions for concrete tasks, among which is the K model, with shortened barrel and free of buttstock, and the SD (Schalldämpfer),

Concealed
The K model can be concealed either in a case with an activator in its handle for firing the gun, or in another type of case which is attached to the grip of the gun and falls away when the gun is needed, its grip remaining in the user's hand.

Modern
The latest MP5 submachine guns are equipped with a modified pistol grip that allows firing in semiautomatic single shot mode, in controlled bursts of two or three rounds, and in free bursts. The modes are controlled by pressing on the grip with the index finger.

HECKLER UND KÖCH SUBMACHINE GUNS

TACTICAL HANDGUARD

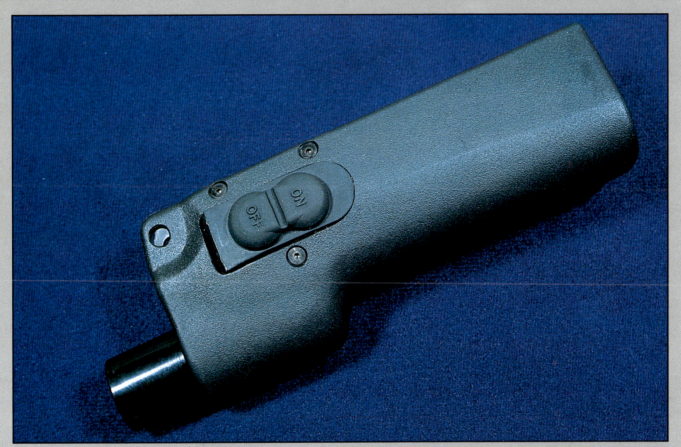

The US firm Laser Products, like others on the market, produces a handguard that can replace the one that originally comes with standard MP5s. The process involves simply removing the two pins that hold the original component in place and replacing it with the new one, affixing it with the pins. The operation is carried out in a few seconds and allows the easy activation of diverse sight and vision equipment, such as Sure-Fire L60 flashlights and sights, among which is the laser model L70 operating at 670 nanometers.

This is possible because the handguard has an activator on its right side that allows the flashlight to be turned on and off according to need, by just pressing on the area with the left hand fingers, the laser that makes instinctive aiming easier also being activated in the same manner. This accessory is used by the great majority of police assault groups in the world. Recently, new models have appeared on the market, such as those presented by Brüguer & Thomet in Paris in November, 1999, which can be combined with a silencer coupled to the muzzle.

that includes a silencer built around its barrel, which is shorter than the basic model, despite the fact that the length of the silencer makes it appear longer. This model can be obtained in the two buttstock variations.

The continuous needs expressed by their customers led H&K to design carrying cases for the K variant; a new model with an outer finish that is more resistant to rust, designated with the letter N, for Navy, to indicate that it was requested by the US Navy; versions with a pistol grip that offer the possibility of firing in controlled bursts; products modified to fire the potent 10x25 mm Auto cartridge or its reduced load variant, the .40 Smith & Wesson; and the K model, equipped with a laterally folding buttstock designed for aircraft pilots.

Remarkable characteristics

These weapons are known for their reliability and durability, and for their great capacity for adapting to all types of needs, as they take advantage of the characteristics offered by the numerous accessories on the market. Among the accessories available for most models of

HECKLER UND KÖCH SUBMACHINE GUNS

Integrated silencer
The SD line includes a cylindrical element on the front end with inner chambers designed to act as a silencer and reduce the report produced when the arm is fired, especially when used with subsonic bullets.

this line are clips to link two or three cartridges so that more ammunition is available, silencers placed on regular muzzles with various systems for attachment, sight bases for attaching to the upper part of the gun for mounting different types of sights, among which is a low-profile aluminum sight introduced as the result of collaboration with the Swedish firm Aimpoint and the Swiss firm Brügger & Thomet, ultra-compact lasers that can be stored in the small front compartment designed for cleaning implements, and handguards modified to serve as activators for illuminating flashlights or lasers.

These complements improve the weapon's performance, keeping it in the lead for weapons of this type. Also contributing to this, despite the many years which have passed since it was designed and first put into production, its semi-rigid lock with roller mechanism and light weight continue functioning perfectly without jamming, allowing full reliability, although the mark it leaves on the shell is very characteristic.

Also remarkable is the durability and toughness of the materials used to manufacture the product, especially the embossed steel sheet used for the body and the magazine rim area, with the buttstock and handguard being particularly tough, as they are made of a plastic derivative. The retractile buttstock is very solid as well, holding up against the rough treatment users give it, extending it and retracting it as the situation demands.

Maintenance is quite simple because of the three pins which allow the various modules of the submachine gun to be taken apart for cleaning or revision of inner parts without the need for tools. The process of disassembling the integrated silencer that comes with the SDs is also easy, and it can be easily cleaned with compressed air.

Finally, another interesting feature is its weight, which ranges from 2 kg for the K variant to 3.5 kg for the SD equipped with metallic buttstock, and its length, which ranges from 35 cm for the smallest version to 78 cm for the SD6 with fixed buttstock.

Aiming
The four mounts on the upper body allow various models of sight bases to be attached, on which can be affixed holographic, red dot or optical sights, depending on the user's preferences.

SPECIAL POLICE GROUP OF THE ARGENTINE GENDARMES

In 1985, the National Police Corps of the Republic of Argentina was entrusted with maintaining the physical safety of passengers at international airports in Argentina, a mission which requires them to be prepared to handle anything from small incidents with passengers to high risk situations involving hostages held in aircraft.

As there was no police group capable of handling the latter type of circumstance, especially those involving terrorist groups, it was decided to create a special police group with specially trained personnel and sophisticated weapons and equipment.

Process of creation

For this reason, after the approval of Resolution No. 499/86 of the Ministry of Defense, the Special Forces Section of the National Police Corps of Argentina was created on May 30, 1986. A group of officers and non-commissioned officers were sent to Spain and France, where they studied the Special Assault Unit (Unidad Especial de Intervención, or UEI) of the Spanish Guardia Civil and the French Groupement d'Intervention de la Gendarmerie Nationale (GIGN), respectively, receiving basic training and general orientation of how they operate during their stay with both groups.

This experienced helped them to consolidate their Section and begin the training courses for members and the process of acquiring the necessary equipment for their activities. They began to carry out missions in 1989.

Varied missions
Their organizational structure consists of a Head of Section, a Support Group, the GEDEX Group and the Assault Section, with four Assault Groups each consisting of assault and

Extraction
Spie rig is a technique in which a group of officers wear a harness that they attach to a rope with snap rings. A helicopter pulls them up with the rope and allows the team to evacuate a specific point very quickly.

Travel
The Police Force has been assigned Ecureuil helicopters, made by the French firm Aerospatiale, which are used for special operations requiring this means for transporting the members of assault groups, either inside or hanging from the skids.

SPECIAL POLICE GROUP OF THE ARGENTINE GENDARMES

response teams, whose principal mission is to handle any dangerous or delicate situation that transcends the capacity of regular police forces, especially in cases in which armed resistance is expected, for reasons of economy of strength and to increase the chances of success.

In order to be able to take on these important duties, the members of the Assault Groups are qualified in techniques and tactics that allow them to carry out the following: operate on the ground in cases of hijacking, saving the hostages, means and facilities involved in the emergency from any danger; recover public or private facilities occupied by various types of groups with different aims who put up armed resistance; and act in support of the Security Squadrons of the National Police Corps to provide high-level, short-term protection for persons or nuclear materials transport in concrete situations whose importance would advise against the use of regular forces.

Training
The training of a special unit is based on a rigorous selection process, correct training and continuous practice with diverse exercises that allow the officers to be prepared for the missions they will be entrusted.

By the same token, the Special Forces Section can support operations of citizen control in cases of social unrest that require a show of force, neutralization of dangerous points of armed resistance, and rapid and conclusive action on specific targets. They are also in charge of providing custody for VIPs whose safety is temporarily the responsibility of the VIP Protection Force, and of providing security during the transfer of very dangerous prisoners.

Additional activities
The previously-mentioned activities are complemented with operations such as air transport infiltration on isolated drug trafficking and/or terrorist groups, supporting intelligence forces in their activities involving dangerous criminals,

Compact
The Heckler und Köch MP5K submachine gun is a very compact weapon that fires bursts of 9x19 millimeter Parabellum cartridges at a rate of approximately one thousand shots per minute, and its principle feature is its facility for being concealed under a jacket or in a briefcase.

and actively cooperating with similar units from other countries, in particular those countries belonging to Mercosur, in legal actions against international organized crime groups who endanger the common security of one or more countries.

They are also in charge of training personnel who are to join the Section, as well as those who require special trai-

SPECIAL POLICE GROUP OF THE ARGENTINE GENDARMES

ning regarding techniques specific to certain special operations, should the need arise.

The GEDEX Group is basically in charge of all special activities dealing with handling and deactivation of explosive, incendiary and/or toxic devices or materials, with the aim of eliminating or limiting their effects in order to protect the people and materials that could be affected, permanently supporting the operations of the Assault Section.

Their support duties cover: searching and locating regulation or improvised explosive devices and explosive, incendiary and/or toxic materials; removing and transporting these devices or materials and deactivating, neutralizing or destroying them; drawing up reports as well as expert and technical investigation reports on aspects related to explosive and incendiary materials in states previous and subsequent to explosion; and acting in coordination with the Police Force's Center of Instruction on Explosives in specific courses, supporting the development and improvement of the instruction given through diverse means.

Argentine
The Special Forces Section is an elite Argentine police group consisting of people selected and trained to handle all missions requiring special skills and involving a high risk level.

Selection of personnel

Those who voluntarily apply to become members of this Section must be officers or non-commissioned officers, and it is an honor and a great responsibility to be chosen to join this force.

Highly prepared
The officers are psychologically prepared for handling both their rigorous initial training as well as their daily routine work. Their physical training is based on increasing their strength, endurance and flexibility. They must be able to run ten kilometers with all of their equipment in less than 45 minutes, carry out ten pull ups, over 50 pushups and 80 sit-ups, go through the combat course in less than 3 minutes and 50 seconds, and perfectly master the techniques of swimming and scuba diving.

Because their preparation in the techniques of handling firearms is of vital impor-

Parachuting
The members of this assault group are also qualified for parachuting, an excellent means of reaching the most remote areas with speed, which is fundamental, considering the enormous geographical area occupied by Argentina.

SPECIAL POLICE GROUP OF THE ARGENTINE GENDARMES

M24 SWS PRECISION RIFLE

M24 SWS (Sniper Weapon System) is the name of a variant of the Remington bolt-operated 700 model that has been modified by the addition of an HS precision butt stock, a potent sight and other small changes in its configuration.

The weapon, also adopted by U.S. Army snipers and many US SWAT teams, is the modified version of a rifle originally designed for hunting. Its outstanding features are its very smooth manual operation, and because its built-in magazine can hold six 7.62x51 mm cartridges. To improve its precision, it is equipped with an improved firing mechanism, a heavy barrel with five inner riflings, a attachment on the lower butt stock for a bipod and a high-quality optical sight.

Its basic specifications are: weight without the sight of 5.49 kilograms; length of 1.092 meters; initial speed of 792 meters per second and maximum effective range of 800 meters.

tance, they practice daily and are required to fire a minimum of 200 shots per week with short weapons and the same amount with long weapons, with a minimum of 95 % effectiveness. Despite their special preparation, which allows them to shoot an opponent shielded behind a hostage with only a small part of their body showing, they operate on the assumption that neutralization prevails over elimination.

Additionally, they also carry out exercises in scuba diving and parachuting, and must know the specific techniques involved in using compressed air bottles and closed circuit oxygen systems, or in using both manual and automatically opening parachutes. There is a small group specialized in aerial infiltration over small areas and another group of frogmen for amphibious operations. To complement the training they receive at their training centers, which serves as their base, they also travel to other countries to carry out similar joint operations –such as the trip they recently made to Brazil to share experiences with a similar group from that country– or receive visits from a variety of units, such as the United States Special Forces, joint work that allows constant improvement.

The GEDEX members follow a more specific training program, with a course structured similarly to the Spanish one. Personnel having passes the physical, technical, psychological and medical examinations go through a training stage lasting approximately sixty days on Searching and Locating (S&L), and then a second stage of similar duration to train them as Deactivation Specialist (*Técnico en Desactivación*, or TEDAX).

Aspiring candidates must have served for at least three years in the Police Force, and only 40 % of those who begin training

SPECIAL POLICE GROUP OF THE ARGENTINE GENDARMES

manage to finish it. Before they reached operative capacity on December 3, 1988, they had to attend the TEDAX School of the Guardia Civil Police Corps in Spain, the Police Academy of the State of Louisiana, the Military Base of the State of Virginia and the National Police School of Deactivation in Peru. The GEDEX directs the Center for Instruction on Explosives, where they train their own personnel, various Argentine military and police force personnel, and similar personnel from Brazil, Uruguay, Peru and France.

Varied equipment

These officers work in dark body suits, wearing face masks and protective gear on their torsos and heads, and flexible, comfortable boots. In addition to this, they also have the camouflage uniforms used by snipers, scuba diving equipment and parachuting equipment, including both MC1 1C automatic parachutes and manual ones such as XL Cloud and Hércules.

Assault

These Argentine police officers practice continually in controlled situations that simulate reality. This scenario, in which the officers are wearing gas masks and are using real fire, simulates an assault on a house where terrorists are holding several hostages.

Regarding weaponry, each member is assigned a Sig Sauer P226 semiautomatic pistol and a Smith & Wesson revolver chambered to fire .38 Special/357 Magnum and equipped with either a 2 1/2 or 4 inch barrel, depending on the user's preference. The operative groups are equipped with the excellent MP5 submachine guns manufactured by the German firm Heckler und Köch (H&K), of which they use version A3 with retractable butt stock, the SD3 with integrated silencer, and the compact model, K.

The snipers are equipped with M24 SWS (Sniper Weapon System) bolt-

Manual paratroopers

A small group of these officers is qualified for parachuting using the manual method. This type of parachuting requires mastery of a technique that allows great precision in landing on very small target areas, such as the roof of a building or a courtyard.

action rifles, of 7.62x51 mm (.308 Winchester) caliber and the Sig Sauer SSG 2000, which takes the same ammunition as the former weapon, and the Barrett M82A1 semiautomatic rifle fed with magazines holding 10 12.70x99 mm (.50 Browning) caliber cartridges. Other weapons available to them include: Valtro 12/70 caliber slide-operated shotguns, single shot H&K grenade launchers that fire various types of 40 millimeter ammunition, among which are smoke bombs for concealment and tear gas, Belgian medium-sized FN MAG machine guns and 60mm light Israeli mortars.

Accessories include visible and infrared laser illuminators for MP5s, day optical sights and optronic sights that amplify residual light, night vision goggles, day and night observation sights, armored shields for protection during advance, stun grenades and a robot equipped with sensors and radar that can move through buildings to observe and collect all sorts of information.

SPECIAL POLICE GROUP OF THE ARGENTINE GENDARMES

Collaboration
The elite Unit of the Argentine Police Corps maintains contact with various similar units, whether military or police, in other countries, and receives visits from delegations interested in learning about their organization and materials. This group from Asia is interested in the materials used by the GEDEX.

GEDEX members are assigned a very complete set of specialized personal equipment in the categories of investigation, illumination, protection, observation, weapons, auxiliary equipment and transportation. The first area includes electronic stethoscopes, parabolic and directional microphones, portable x-ray equipment and analyzing chambers for explosive gases. They also use dogs trained to detect explosives.

The category of illumination includes spotlights, reflectors and special flashlights. Protective gear includes explosion-proof blankets and thick protective uniforms for the removal and deactivation of explosive devices. Observation equipment includes sights and binoculars, and the weaponry includes a water gun that shoots water at very high pressure. They also use RO-VEH remote-control robots and blue armored trucks for carrying all of the equipment needed by these specialists.

Deactivation experts
The GEDEX members are assigned a complete set of personal protective gear. They travel in blue armored trucks that can carry various systems and employ remote-controlled, caterpillar-track robots.

ATF SPECIAL AGENTS

In the United States government, the distribution of the different administrative tasks is very hierarchical. Those relating to the control of alcohol, tobacco and firearms are assigned to the Bureau of Alcohol, Tobacco and Firearms of the Treasury Department.

This control function is exercised by officers stationed in the Bureau's different headquarters established in major cities. These officers have been trained in investigation and handling of personal firearms in specific schools such as the Federal Law Enforcement Training Center in Glynco, Georgia, where they follow the program of the Criminal Investigator School, which lasts nine weeks, and the New Professional Training, where they gain the preparation necessary to carry out the tasks entrusted the institution, directed by John W. Magaw.

Special groups

Once the officers have taken up a position as a TEA (Treasury Enforcement Agent), they can be assigned to the headquarters in Washington DC or any of the various regional offices in different states. They then begin to carry out different tasks, depending on their specific qualifications, which include completion of a four-year diploma before joining the agency.

Firing power
The Sig Sauer P226 semiautomatic pistol is a very powerful weapon that fires 9x19 millimeter Parabellum bullets, standing out for its excellent finish, for the 15-cartridge capacity of its magazines and for its great reliability.

Professional selection

Those agents having demonstrated in their activities skills and personal qualities that are above the norm, and perform outstandingly in the quarterly qualification examinations verifying their preparation for handling the assigned firearms, can request to be assigned to a special group.

The first step they must take is to fill out some forms with their personal and professional data. Candidates selected from the information on the forms are given psychological tests. Those who perform best follow specific training at specialized centers that program intensive courses that last six weeks, during which the agents attend theoretical classes and carry out practical exercises in subjects such as tactical maneuvers, per-

ATF SPECIAL AGENTS

sonal protection, handling special weapons, using explosives, surveillance and arrests, special equipment and a great many other things providing them the knowledge that allows them to join the special units, which were formed at the beginning of the 90s.

These groups, five of which are constantly active, are called Special Response Teams (SRT) and are located in the different zones throughout the United States to make their capacity for response more effective. Each one consists of nearly fifty agents working independently, or collectively when the situation so requires. They meet four times a year for one week of training in which a forty hour program is covered to promote rapport for joint missions and to improve their skills by teaching new techniques and knowledge on the latest equipment.

These officers often carry out a specific task in the city where they are posted, which is related to the investigation tasks assigned to the ATF Bureau. The groups specialized in special response, which vary in each city, so that in Atlanta, for example, there are four and in Miami 15, work in the most varied activities in their respective cities. The meet as a group to support their colleagues in activities that involve higher risk. Teams from different cities are also brought together to meet concrete needs in operations which are believed to be more dangerous or require a great number of agents, and on occasions, an entire SRT works together.

Greater preparation

For very concrete needs regarding agent response capacity or the need for immediate deployment, there is a sixth SRT integrated into the Special Operations Division at the headquarters in Washington, whose personnel is more highly qualified because they work only on police operations such as assaults or detentions, and are assigned higher level equipment than the rest of the special units. There are specialists called "advanced observers" who support the teams: They carry out the task of gathering all sorts of information often having to do with tactical intelligence, a mission

Capacity
The ATF's Special Response Teams consist of select agents who have received training in accordance with the special missions they are expected to carry out. When their support is not required, these officers carry out regular police duties.

Tactical holster
The holster for carrying the 9x19 millimeters Parabellum Sig Sauer semiautomatic pistol that the agents use as a secondary weapon is normally placed on the outer thigh. The pistol is used on those occasions when it is required as a complement to a submachine gun or assault rifle.

ATF SPECIAL AGENTS

AR-15A2 ASSAULT RIFLE

This assault rifle is manufactured by the US firm Colt Firearms at their Hartford, Connecticut plant, although the license to produce these arms has ended up in the hands of various manufacturers throughout the world. It was originally designed as a military weapon, but it has been adopted by Police Departments in many states due to its low cost, the fact that it fires ammunition sufficiently potent for the activity for which it is used and is very simple to use by personnel with minimum training. In the ATF, both the standard AR-15A2 variant and the M4 Carbine version are used, both of which are acquired in their civilian versions, which include a mode selector that only allows single shot or semiautomatic use in order to gain greater precision and eliminate the possibility of firing in bursts. The A2 variant is equipped with a heavy barrel, fixed buttstock made of synthetic material and sights that allow effective fire within a 300 meter range, while the M4 has a folding buttstock, smaller handguard and shorter barrel.
They both fire 5.56x45 millimeter cartridges in magazines with a capacity of 30 rounds, the rifle weighing 3.4 kilograms and the carbine 2.52.

which requires them to survey the territory before their colleagues act, or at the same time. While carrying out their functions, which sometimes involve armed conflict with the people they monitor, they carry 7.62x51 millimeter caliber precision rifle with a range of up to 500 meters.

The preparation of these special units has been promoted recently, after the disastrous mission they carried out to capture the members of a sect led by David Koresh. They had retired to a ranch near the city of Waco, Texas and, heavily armed, these "visionaries" responded by firing all sorts of arms against the initial assault carried out by the ATF's SRT specialists, who were caught in the fire and were forced to retreat, leaving many injured people and several dead among their ranks, despite the fact that their professional qualifications should have allowed them to carry out the operation without problems.

The incident finally ended with the intervention of other governmental agencies and with a fire caused by the tear gas bombs thrown at the sect members to cause them to desist. Despite all of their efforts, dozens of men, women and children died.

Strategic plan

The Treasury Department is responsible for collecting taxes, training security forces, insuring compliance with industrial regulations and preventing or reducing violent crime when it is related to alcohol, tobacco or firearms. Moreover, they are in charge of arresting suspects if the District Attorney's Office so requests, and support the Secret Service in the protection of dignitaries or politicians.

ATF SPECIAL AGENTS

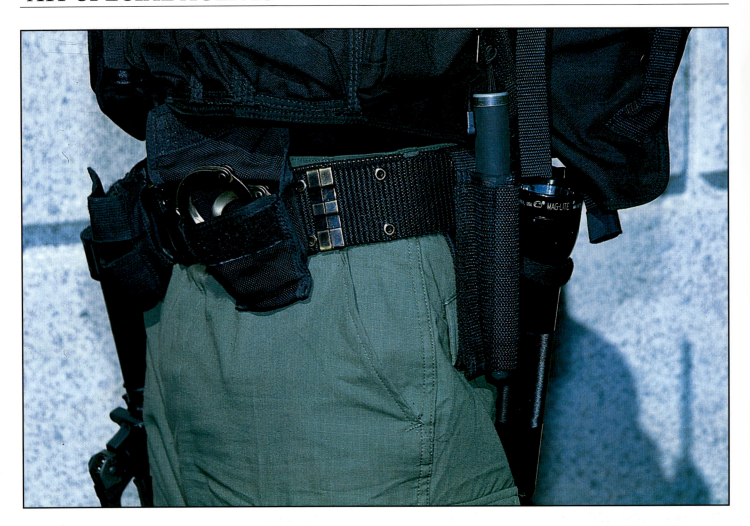

Accessories
The belt is used to carry various accessories so that they are on hand should they be necessary. These include the ASP telescopic nightstick that can be easily extended, handcuffs and MagLite flashlights, which provide much light and can also be used as clubs.

Varied armaments

These activities, carried out especially by members of the SRTs, which are more qualified and better equipped to handle special risk situations, require the use of a varied range of arms adapted to every mission and period in concrete.

The basic weapon of these men is the assault rifle, of which they use AR-15A2 and M4 Carbine models, manufactured by the US firm Colt Firearms. These weapons, chambered for the use of potent 5.56x45 mm (.223 Remington) caliber ammunition of Federal Tactical Application Police (TAP) type, designed to combine the necessary precision and perforation for police needs. They are fed with curved magazines with a capacity for 30 cartridges and stand out for having been modified to fire only in semiautomatic mode or shot by shot, in order to gain greater precision and eliminate bursts of fire, which are harder to control and can hit civilians who are near the scene of the armed confrontation.

The former Colt model has a 20 inch barrel and a buttstock made of synthetic material that make it larger and lend it greater precision at medium range, while the latter is equipped with a shorter barrel and a retractable buttstock, which makes it more compact and easy to transport. The assigned submachine gun is also

Facial protection
On occasions when tear gas or smoke bombs are used, a gas mask becomes essential to allow the agents to breath and move comfortably. An interesting feature is the location of the filter cartridge, placed on the side to allow the user to aim rifles more easily.

ATF SPECIAL AGENTS

compact –the Heckler und Köch MP5A4 of 9x19 mm Parabellum caliber, equipped with a fixed buttstock and has been optimized with a Laser Products H28 handguard, with an activator for a potent L60 Sure-Fire flashlight with which to illuminate dark areas for improved detection of criminals, thus improving its excellent precision.

This specific model is complemented by the MP5A5 with retractile buttstock, and both use a firing mechanism linked to a selector on the side of the weapon which allows the selection of the single shot mode or controlled bursts of only two shots. Their official ammunition is of the Federal Hidra Sock type, that includes a 147 grain hollow tip that stands out for its partial metallic blanket and its capacity for deformation to increase the capacity for tearing into clothes or body tissue.

This same type of cartridge is used in P226 pistols by the firm Sig Sauer that the agents normally carry as an auxiliary

Constant training
The members of the ATF's SRTs meet periodically to carry out complex training to homogenize group capacity and to provide a positive influence on the personal training of each individual.

weapon in an Eagle leg holster. They are normally fed with 15 to 30 round cartridges. As a complement to this weapon and for covert activities, they can also use P225, P228 and P239 or Smith & Wesson 640 model revolvers, of which they use both the .38 Special and the .357 Magnum.

On certain occasions, Remington 870 slide-operated shotguns can also be useful. They take 12/70 caliber cartridges loaded with double zero pellets or slug bullets. High-precision shots are fired with Remington 700 rifles, using .308 Winchester ammunition, 3.5-10X50 mm Leupold Tactical Police Vari-X III optical day sights and Simrad Optronics KN202 optronic night modules.

Personal gear
Their gear includes green BDU (Battle Dress Uniform) type military pants, navy blue shirts to cover the torso and Eagle tactical jackets worn over the shirts. The latter serve to transport the accessories necessary for their tasks, as well as half a dozen magazines or stun grenades, and also constitutes a personal protective device because it is made of Kevlar fiber so that it meets the standards of a Class III bulletproof vest. Their heads are protected with PASGT model Kevlar helmets covered with a black coating.

Tactical jacket
Normally, a tactical assault jacket is worn over a bulletproof vest. Its multiple pockets allow such elements as a radio, stun grenades, cartridges for personal weapons, gas masks and a small first aid kit to be carried comfortably and rationally.

Their special and modern equipment also includes: tactical or military boots, gas masks with the filter on the left to facilitate aiming long weapons, Motorola Securenet Saber communications equipment, Oakley safety glasses, MiniMaglite flashlights, elbow and knee pads to protect these areas, ASP telescopic nightsticks, protective gloves, combat trucks for transporting the teams, protective shields and a long list of other elements.

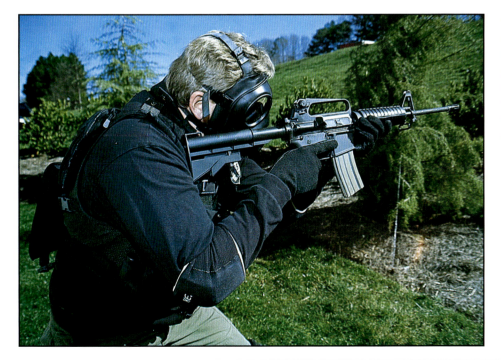

INDEX

Geo: Spanish Police Corps Assault Group 4
Personal protective gear 14
NOCS: Italian Special Police 20
Communications systems 30
Phoenix PD Special Response Team 34
Snipers 45
The Special Operations Section of Atlanta 53
Specialized vehicles 63
Czech Special Police 69
Heckler und Koch submachine guns 79
Special Police Group of the Argentine Gendarmes 85
ATF Special Agents 91
Index 96